FINDING YOUR EDGE

Katrina
Enjoy life and do well
Carl Schtt

Swan Kay

FINDING YOUR EDGE

SUCCESS SECRETS FROM TOP 16 BUSINESS THINKERS

DENISE O'NEILL

Printed in the United States of America.
Library of Congress Control Number: 2019938960
ISBN: 978-1-949639-90-2

Book Design: Melanie Cloth

TABLE OF CONTENTS

SYNOPSIS

If you're a small- or middle-market business owner, you're under a distinctive sort of pressure. Staying on top of the day-to-day needs of your company while looking ahead and retaining lessons from the past. Keeping an eye on the healthcare premiums, regulations, and payroll needs of today, along with the labor availability, fuel prices, and market trends of tomorrow. You know the challenge of balancing your family's present financial needs with the growth needs of a company that you hope will benefit your family for years to come. But you also know the distinctive rewards.

Here at The Alternative Board (TAB), we work with many leaders of small to midsize businesses from every background you can imagine. In our supporting role of owners and CEOs from fields ranging from accounting to architecture, we've recognized that there is no one formula to success. However, we have seen some important trends.

In this anthology, sixteen exceptional business leaders share the lessons that have shaped their success. It is our hope that, through reading their stories, you will discover new ways to run your own business smoothly and effectively, minimizing the pressures and maximizing the one-of-a-kind rewards.

INTRODUCTION

Small- and middle-market business owners are unique. They fall somewhere between the industrial giants of our time and "two Chucks with a truck." They worry about payroll. They worry about contracts, healthcare premiums, suppliers, subcontractors, regulations, and finding good staff. They come from backgrounds as diverse as engineering, accounting, and architecture. Some started out as electrical or mechanical contractors.

For their vast differences, something they tend to have in common is that even as they remain engrossed in the present—extinguishing and preventing multiple fires each day—they also reflect critically on the past. They do this so that the ghost of past failures will not have the chance to slow them down.

At the same time, they challenge themselves to look forward. What will the market be like next year? Will fuel prices be up or down? Will borrowing money be easier or more difficult? Will local, regional, domestic, and international markets behave next year as they're behaving now? Will workforce trends change? Will there be shortages in specialty labor?

Heaped on top of these normal business concerns, for small- and middle-market leaders, is a profound concern about the personal and family aspects of the business. When family is involved, they find themselves considering not only the current impact of the business, but also how it could affect future generations. They're constantly balancing their own financial needs with those of the company.

The business leaders who share their stories on the following pages are creative thinkers. They have faced the concerns outlined above with logic, determination, innovation, and a perennial willingness to learn—and they have come out ahead. These leaders manage current operations while leading their companies into the future. Intelligent and thoughtful, they demonstrate the rare ability of managing both present and future curves of the business, without forgetting lessons from the past.

None of them have gone it alone. Most have succeeded by building organizations and teams that span geographies, lines of businesses, and competencies as well as product and service offerings. They additionally know the value of seeking outside support and consultation when necessary. We at The Alternative Board, or TAB, have been fortunate enough to serve as part of a support network for the leaders whose stories fill this book.

The business leaders who share their stories on the following pages are creative thinkers. They have faced the concerns outlined above with logic, determination, innovation, and a perennial willingness to learn—and they have come out ahead.

Having worked with so many small- and middle-market business owners and CEOs, we recognize there isn't one single formula for success. Some of our leaders are highly educated; others never set foot in a college. Some speak with a

New England private school cadence, while others rattle along in the vernacular of their region. Some come from money, but most don't. Some are introverted, and others are constantly out and about.

We do, however, see trends. Each leader seems to have an approach, an operating model, or a way of conducting business that works for them, their employees, their customers, and their market. They have the ability to build a guiding team and coalesce more and more people to be a part of their journey.

What we've collected for your enjoyment are the best practices of sixteen of these business leaders. A sampling of their secret sauce. The lessons that have brought them great success. Because they believe in collaboration and sharing best practices, they're sharing them with you.

We thank these market leaders for their efforts and selflessness. We also hope that, as you read, you will take away a few gems that will help you lead your own business to ever greater success.

SURVIVING AN ECONOMIC DOWNTURN AS A MIDSIZE BUSINESS

LISA GOBRECHT, PRESIDENT, DMW

I always tell people that at Daft McCune Walker (DMW) we design the dirt. We're a land development consulting firm, meaning, in practical terms, a business of civil engineers, landscape architects, and surveyors. Whereas traditional architects design buildings and other vertical structures, we design horizons—the ground beneath, as well as the infrastructure, that supports the aboveground project.

DMW was incorporated in 1970. I've been with the company since the late eighties. I first started at DWM as a clerk, after three years working in retail following college. And now, almost thirty years later, I'm president of the company.

What's unique about my story is that I'm not an engineer, a landscape architect, or a surveyor. I'm not one of the technical people. I came through the accounting-administrative-management side of the house. Clerk to accounting manager to CFO to president.

In our industry, people normally excel based on their technical ability; this is a historical tendency in the leadership structure of the industry. Throughout the first forty or so years of DMW's existence, the president of the company was either a landscape architect or an engineer. I was the first person who didn't come from that technical side.

In our industry, people normally excel based on their technical ability; this is a historical tendency in the leadership structure of the industry.

While I didn't necessarily have technical experience, I did have business acumen and an understanding of how to manage the company. I believe this has helped us to make decisions more clearly. When you're making calls about what's best for your business, it can be easy to get caught up in sentimental thinking.

"But this is a great project," someone will say.

"But this is a client we've been working with for fifteen years," adds a seasoned veteran.

Instead of getting pulled into that way of looking at things, I can be objective. That kind of black-and-white reasoning, limiting the gray areas, helps companies thrive.

When I became president in 2010, we were still experiencing an economic downturn that had hit the construction and building industry hard. Over the previous approximately two years, the company had gone from about seventy people to roughly forty. It was a difficult time, to say the least.

Currently, we are a team of forty-seven. And while our numbers haven't increased greatly since that economic downturn, we have grown in terms of revenue since I took the reins. What I've observed during previous recessions has held true—when you're figuring out how to do more with less, the technology tends to jump in and take hold.

The harsh reality of technological shifts is that when you evolve due to the incorporation of new technology, you will often end up needing fewer bodies. We've seen this in many industries and it has certainly proved true in our case—at one point we had twelve to fourteen people in the field; today we have four to five. But we feel the pressure from both sides: reduced or commoditized fees and a smaller workforce filling needed positions. We recognized many years ago the gaps that would be created by people leaving the industry—and young people not joining—and identified how technology could fill the void. Being able to face this type of change, openly and realistically, has enabled us not only to survive but also to shine in a very competitive field.

> *The harsh reality of technological shifts is that when you evolve due to the incorporation of new technology, you will often end up needing fewer bodies.*

Aside from readily adapting new technology and making the corresponding necessary staffing changes, the factor that has most contributed to our ongoing success is what every great company must have: a good reputation. If we didn't have that, we wouldn't have survived as long as we have—or created the legacy that continues on.

We're proactive about our reputation. For us, this means being selective about the clients we work with, the projects we take on, and the staff we bring on board. It also means staying on top of trends pertinent to the industry. In our field, there's been growing attention in the last decade or so to stormwater management. It's something people care about and it falls in our domain; therefore, we need to understand it thoroughly.

This doesn't mean we need to be the first to jump on the latest-trend bandwagon; we only need to stay well-informed, keeping a finger on the pulse of our industry, and always be prepared to discuss and answer our clients' questions. This enables us to position ourselves as knowledgeable, up-to-date experts whom our clients can trust without hesitation.

There is a notion in business management that it's necessary to be on the cutting edge, to be leaders in whatever the hot topic of the day is. In our decades of experience, we've found that this simply is not the case. Business leaders always need to be informed, but we also need to assess the size and regional scope of our companies—and to be realistic. Are we going to lead the way in every new industry trend? No. Are we going to have a well-informed position on the ones that matter? Absolutely.

We're very fortunate that our clients come back to us year after year, and I like to attribute that to the fact that we've long recognized that the business world is all about relationships. Business leaders need to remember that while the world may be very big, the world of their industries can be surprisingly small.

This is why it is important—always—to do right by every customer and be up front and honest with anyone who trusts us enough to provide for their needs. The principle behind this is simple: conduct yourself in a way you can be proud of at all times.

Maybe the networking event you have to attend falls on a day that is particularly bad for you. You're feeling under the weather, you have family matters on your mind, you're stressed over the next day's business meeting, or your car started squealing on the ride over. Whatever the case may be, when you walk through that door, you need to do so with a genuine smile on your face. The next person you meet could be your number-one client three years down the road.

Evolving, and being proactive about your reputation, may seem like unrelated matters, but they really go hand in hand. When your clients transition, you transition. This is how clients come to know you—not only as a business they enjoyed working with initially, but also as a competent fit to serve their needs in the present, and in the future.

Our industry, like many, comprises both very large and very small engineering firms; the middle market has somewhat disappeared. For the handful of us who have not only held on but succeeded, a key has been to recognize what's currently important in the industry and realistically assess how our company can intersect with that demand.

Recently, for instance, we have added a new chapter of clients from the public side. This is because currently there's an overwhelming focus on environmental issues, particularly stormwater management. Our services are no different from the ones we were providing ten years ago, but because we recognized the increasing importance of a particular issue, we were able to look at who the stakeholders were and how we fit in, ultimately expanding our customer base.

What everyone doesn't realize about the midmarket is that we have competition from both sides. The large companies clearly have resources and a reach that smaller companies don't. But we also have to compete with the small businesses—generally on price and schedule, because they can have a staff of ten, very little overhead, and impressive flexibility.

What everyone doesn't realize about the midmarket is that we have competition from both sides.

Our job is to show our clients why we make more sense than either of their other options. If we're going to charge 5 to 10 percent more than the small guy, then we need to be prepared to show our clients what they're getting for that cost increase. And at times, large companies seem to have limitless resources, enabling them to present an all-encompassing program that can be appealing to any client.

Another meaningful necessity for surviving and thriving—one I would say doesn't typically get its due—is keeping strong financial records. The company has to support itself, and if revenues are dropping while labor costs are rising, then we have to sit down and make tough decisions in a timely manner.

Nobody likes acting on the hard decisions, especially if one involves a team member. But by not making the tough decisions quickly, you end up hurting your company's long-term success. For that reason, it's important not only to make the difficult decisions— but to act on them quickly.

As an owner who comes from the accounting side, and as someone who's been through a couple of economic downturns with the company already, I watch certain financial metrics. When these metrics begin to fluctuate, I work to find out what's causing the change—and then make decisions based on that.

There have probably been a few times when we waited a month or so too long to act, but it's never gone far beyond that. I attribute my adoption of this policy to my mentors. The people who led the company before me had strong convictions about not letting things slide. If, for instance, they found themselves putting personal money into the business in order to keep it going, then it was time for a change—immediately.

As I mentioned, we watch certain trending numbers—monthly, quarterly, and annually. We monitor them in good times and in bad. The best advice I could give to any business leader would be to find out what those key indicators are for your company and make sure your accounting manager or CFO is regularly reporting those numbers to you.

While I'm a fervent advocate of making sure you're as prepared as possible, I would also advise you not to beat yourself up. When you recognize a problem—and the solution seems obvious—it may be tempting think, "If only I had recognized this two months ago," or, "How can I be implementing this solution only now?" That's not productive. It's best to acknowledge the problem, acknowledge what needs to be done about it, and then act. In other words: Move on. There's zero value to you or your company in raking yourself over the coals.

Listen, we all make mistakes; nobody's perfect. But as an owner, you simply can't spend a lot of time looking back. As the leader of a company, you have to move forward, so your business can as well. It can help to associate yourself with a group of business leaders who have faced similar trials and overcome them. This type of peer resource can help you rally yourself after a minor failure, enabling you to continue moving in the right direction.

As an owner, you simply can't spend a lot of time looking back. As the leader of a company, you have to move forward, so your business can as well.

For me, this mostly boils down to a principle that's at the root of what it means to be a successful business leader—and a happy human being—which is to stay positive. During the last downturn, there was a flood of negative news ... and if you paid too much attention to it, getting sucked into that negativity was easy.

In times like those, it's so important to remember that your company has a future. You must ask yourself, "*When* [not *If*] the economy recovers, how do I want to be positioned?" and, "What do I need to do to be successful *when* that happens?" Realize that this difficult time, too, will pass. Stay positive and keep going.

IT ALL STARTS WITH SALES: FINDING, MOTIVATING, AND REWARDING GREAT SALESPEOPLE

GEORGE HALL, PRESIDENT, LINQ

In 1997, I cofounded Questron, a technology company that sold business phone systems, voice and data cabling, security systems, and home theaters. I successfully sold the company in 2009 but remain involved as president of the board. I am currently the president of another growing technology company, LINQ.

By the age of thirteen, I had no doubts about following in my father's entrepreneurial footsteps. After graduating from Grove City College and earning my master's degree from Johns Hopkins University, I started Questron as a subcontractor in the technology sector. It was a short sprint from that starting point to changing the whole business model and going direct to the consumer. Then I expanded into security—a sector that, at the time, I knew nothing about.

I've always been drawn to technology, specifically because it's so dynamic. It's always changing—and because it never stagnates, it never gets boring. The bad thing about tech, however, is that it's always changing—you have to stay on top of it all the time. My key to staying successful in this ever-evolving field has been to hire people who are smarter than I am.

My two main strengths are management—leading comes naturally to me—and sales. Here's how I look at it: In business, if we don't have sales, we have nothing. You could have the greatest product or service in the world, but if you don't have sales, then you're not going to be able to get your product out to the public and grow your company. It all starts with sales.

For anyone who owns a business or works in upper management and is struggling with sales, I would suggest as a first step defining the kind of salesperson you want: hunter or farmer.

> **You could have the greatest product or service in the world, but if you don't have sales, then you're not going to be able to get your product out to the public and grow your company. It all starts with sales.**

The hunter goes out and finds food. In business terms, this is the person who knocks on doors, networks, and treks through the woods, rooting out what's under the leaves as necessary. A farmer, on the other hand, cultivates the field. In business terms, this translates into cultivating existing clients— keeping them happy—and growing the network by expanding what you're currently selling.

When starting your team, you have to decide what type of salespeople you need. The biggest failure most companies make today is hiring the wrong type. Most business owners understand that they need sales—and therefore need to devote the best team possible to it—but figuring out what constitutes "best" for their circumstance is more complicated.

There are many situations in which you need both hunters and farmers—but it all gets down to knowing your business. You may end up needing multiple people on both the outside and the inside. In my situation, I saw the need primarily for hunters, because we needed food.

The initial reason for our success was sales. The step after sales is support. This is where it's important to understand that everybody in your company is actually in sales, including your support team. Everybody—managers, technicians, admin, and so on—engages with the client in one way or another, meaning that everybody influences whether that client is likely to do business with you in the future.

I often tell people that in business there's a first sale and a second sale. The first comes when the hunter goes out and finds the food. The second sale is the deliverable. In our case, this occurred when the technicians delivered the product. This still qualifies as sales, because the way we presented ourselves to clients determined how they felt about working with us in the future. If our technicians didn't handle the job professionally—if they left a mess, were rude, or simply didn't do the job well—then we're not going to get more business from that sale.

Creating the best sales force possible is a complex process. After you've recruited a great team, it's then your job to help motivate them. The common perception is that salespeople are motivated only by money. And while that's not false—everyone likes to earn money—in the hierarchy of motivation, it probably comes third.

The number-one motivator for members of a sales team is *winning*. The thrill of victory. Excellent salespeople don't just want to win—they *have* to win. They'll do whatever it takes to experience that triumph.

That's one good reason I always like recruiting athletes for my sales force. Sales is an emotional roller coaster. You fail more often than you succeed. Athletes are perfectly primed to handle these ups and downs without throwing in the towel. They understand what it takes to be successful and how hard they have to work. They understand that if Approach X didn't work, then it's time to implement Approach Y.

> **The number-one motivator for members of a sales team is winning. The thrill of victory. Excellent salespeople don't just want to win—they have to win.**

When people bring the competitiveness and resilience that are hallmarks of competitive sports into the workplace, they become the kind of go-getters that are so prized in the business world. They're continually setting strategic goals for themselves, and they don't accept failure—because they need to win.

The second thing that motivates salespeople is recognition. Put simply, after they win, they want people to *acknowledge* that they've won.

The third tier of motivation is the reward for having won. In other words—the money.

I place such emphasis on discovering great salespeople and learning what makes them tick for a reason. While you can build and incentivize a great sales team, you can't *teach* people to sell. Sure, you can impart hints for how to become slightly more effective, but you can't instill the attitude of a good salesperson—that ever-present desire to achieve.

Here's a great quote from football coach Lou Holtz: "Motivation is simple. You eliminate those who are not motivated."

To tap into that motivation and help my team win, we first set challenging but attainable goals. Then we tracked progress toward those goals by posting the numbers. Everybody in the company could see who was winning. If you've found the right salespeople, they thrive on this kind of competition. They'll like knowing the person next to them is selling ... but they'll want to beat that person—and want the entire organization to know it.

In addition to posting the numbers, I made sure we celebrated every win. To get agreement that *everybody* in the organization is in sales, you have to revel in victories with the whole company—not just the sales team.

Another necessity for motivating your team is making sure they're on the same page as you—that they keep the company mission and goals in sight. The first step is, naturally, creating the vision and goals.

From there, to keep my sales team focused on that vision, I would go over a set of pertinent questions in weekly or biweekly meetings. Who are the clients? Who are the prospects? Where are you in the process? How can I help you close that opportunity? What do you need from the company? What do you need from the rest of the team?

I'm a sports guy—football, specifically—so I like to think of sales goals in terms of football's four quarters. We set the yearly goal at the beginning but we truly measure the progress each quarter—and then again at the end of the year.

A long-term goal, such as an annual goal, typically has the built-in reward of a bonus. But you also have to incentivize along the way. Maybe the best salesperson of the month or quarter gets a special prize. If my whole team performs well for the quarter, I might take them out to race electric go-karts, take a boat ride, or enjoy a nice dinner together. The end of the year is too long to wait. It's important to acknowledge wins along the way so you keep your sales staff engaged and they acquire a taste for frequent success.

It's also helpful to keep in mind that what incentivizes one person isn't necessarily going to work for another. You need to understand all the people on your team—especially in terms of their personal motivation factors. You also need to pay close attention to them—about what makes them tick—without hovering over them. You don't want to shadow your employees' every move. Autonomy equals accountability.

An idea that really underscores accountability—and something I teach my team from the very start—is that every one of them is actually an entrepreneur. They are their own business and CEO. True, they work under the company umbrella, but *they* decide how successful they're going to be. In that sense, they are their own bosses.

Everyone in sales needs to know that they can sell as much or as little as they want. To validate that message, you—the person controlling the management side—have to ensure that the right factors are established that will enable their success. If the right product, support, and service are in place, they can drive the rest.

> **An idea that really underscores accountability—and something I teach my team from the very start—is that every one of them is actually an entrepreneur.**

Beyond failing to put together the right sales team, the primary failure of business owners is inadvertently restricting their teams' success. This happens in a number of ways. First, owners expect success to happen overnight or are negligent about building the right support infrastructure. This will hold back their teams. Then, they create problems by looking over their salespeople's shoulders and questioning every decision. Finally, some novice owners don't want their salespeople outshining them—they feel threatened if their salespeople earn "too much" or experience "too many" wins.

I *want* the sales team to make more than I do. If they're more successful than I am, individually, then I couldn't be happier. When they're successful, the company is successful; when the company is successful, I am successful. But notice that I—the owner—come last in this chain.

Having management that encourages them to reach their full potential gives employees ample reason to stay with the company long term—which benefits the company in many ways. Retaining employees saves money; I don't have to retrain and I don't have to inspire all the buy-in again.

Customers buy from people they trust and have confidence in. That's the first step: The customer has to trust the company they're buying from to deliver. Besides this primary consideration, customer motivation can be broken down into four components, which I envision as four blocks.

COMPANY	PRODUCT
SERVICE	PRICE $

The upper-left block is company. Customers decide they like and believe in Company X, so that's the company they want to buy from.

The upper-right corner is product. No matter what your product is, potential customers must like it and judge it to be better than your competitors' products. Or it must fit a need they don't already have a solution for.

The bottom-left block is service. To be firmly on board, customers must see that you're going to deliver the promised product—and then provide the service necessary to help them establish and maintain it. Whether it's a one-time or an ongoing sale, you have to come through on the service and maintenance side if you expect customers to buy from you again.

Then comes the final square—money. If price is the principal consideration, then you're just a commodity. To be successful in sales, you need to eliminate price as the primary reason.

You have to figure out which of the four components is driving your potential customer. I taught my sales force how to do this and they had great success. The key was creating a workplace in which employees felt that our product was a superior one and our company a cool place to represent. Because they genuinely stood behind our service and found our price to be fair, they exuded that positive evaluation. The clients then followed.

I'll be honest—I'm not the secret of my success. It's the people I hired and surrounded myself with. I'll reiterate that I was able to achieve so much because I hired people much smarter than I am: sharp salespeople who were motivated by the cause and were consistently rewarded their efforts.

One of my former employees recently paid me the ultimate compliment. He said he missed Questron because it was one of the only companies he'd been affiliated with where the work didn't feel like work at all—that in itself was its own reward.

UNEXPECTED LEADERSHIP

ANNA GAVIN, PRESIDENT,
FIRELINE CORPORATION

I don't believe most young women envision a career managing a fire protection company. It's not the kind of industry that anyone really seeks out. But it is the kind of business that finds you. And while I was born into the industry, I never expected to take part in it. It took a family tragedy to find myself at the head of the company; it's now hard to imagine life any other way.

The Fireline Corporation was founded by my grandfather in 1947 as a fire extinguisher service and distribution company. Throughout the 1960s and 1970s, he grew the business, expanding into chemical fire-suppression systems. My father took over the company in 1982 and kept the expansion going, making it a one-stop shop for commercial fire protection. He added new products and services, with Fireline providing everything from fire extinguishers to sprinkler systems to fire alarm protection. Essentially, if it alerted you to a fire—or put out a fire—we furnished it.

I began working for the company off and on in 2001, while still a teenager in college. I really had no intention of working in the business. I was studying art history at the University of Maryland, with no clear career plan. Thankfully, encouraged by my father, I took a few business and accounting classes. I worked for Fireline intermittently for the next few years, while still not sure what I wanted to do with my life.

In 2008, my grandfather passed away at the age of ninety-one. My father continued to run the company, but his health also began to slip. In 2009 he passed away, leaving Fireline and my family grieving and without a leader.

My mother and I agreed we had two choices: We could sell the company, or I could lead it. It was barely a choice. Fireline was my family. I couldn't walk away from it—assuming the leadership role was the only real option.

Not sure what else to do, I took the reins at what seemed the worst possible time, just weeks before Christmas. I was twenty-seven years old and had a five-month-old baby at home. The country was in one of the worst recessions in history. Fireline was a $20 million company with about 150 employees. All of them were looking for assurances that everything was going to be okay. Assurances from me, whether I was prepared for that responsibility or not.

At the time, many of the employees were happy I took charge. I'd worked in the company for eight years already, and people were happy to see it stay in the

> **Fireline was a $20 million company with about 150 employees. All of them were looking for assurances that everything was going to be okay. Assurances from me, whether I was prepared for that responsibility or not.**

family—even if I was young and inexperienced. At the same time, they knew I wasn't going to let the business stay as it was—stagnant. I could see that we, as an organization, had grown outside our comfort zone—but hadn't yet adjusted our business practices to accommodate that growth. I wasn't sure how to change this, but I knew something needed to happen.

It became evident that we couldn't operate like a small family business anymore, at least not to the extent we had been. We needed clearly defined controls and processes in place, along with strong managers, more efficient business practices, new technologies, and a plan for growth. Most importantly, we needed the company to be on board to make those changes. And through all of this, we still needed to stay true to the family-business culture that was so important to our success.

But who was I to lead a company? I hadn't earned my position; it had been thrust on me. I was inexperienced. I was young, and a woman surrounded by men. These worries plagued me those first few years.

I took time early on to simply manage, observe, survive, and most importantly, to learn. What kind of leader did I need to become to meet the company goals and fulfill its needs? I knew I needed to be an educated and effective decision maker. I had to learn general business practices and the particulars of financial data, various business metrics, legal risks, and insurance needs. And I needed to learn the human aspects of the business—personality profiles, employee confrontation, and incentives and motivators.

It was during this stage of learning that I realized I could just ask. Many business owners or managers assume they should know everything, but this only closes them off from ideas and opportunities. My advantage was my willingness to admit early on what I didn't know—which went hand in hand with the realization that those around me didn't expect me to know everything right away. I spent plenty of time asking why. "Why do we do this? Why do we do it that way?" This, in turn, opened up a lot of questions from my team, and we made many positive changes as a result.

In some cases, it was important to balance this open, honest desire to learn from others—this willingness to admit what I didn't know—with a clear display of confidence in myself. Sometimes, I had to live by the mantra "fake it till you make it," projecting confidence in the moment and then quickly working to figure things out for next time. Even though everyone knew I was learning, they still needed to see me as a self-assured leader.

So here I was, learning the business, learning my role, doing what I could to make it known that I was going to be a strong leader. But the company was going through major changes. It needed more than me asking the right questions—it needed action. We began working on a long-term strategy plan that would address many of the big-picture challenges.

I interviewed employees, customers, vendors, and my business and industry peers. I wrote and shared a company vision and values statement. I analyzed costs and made timelines. And slowly but surely, I was able to map out a long-term plan. Having that road map was an immediate game changer. I felt I knew where we needed to take the company, where we needed to be to get better, to grow, and to improve. Even today I spend much of my time on this type of planning.

During those first five years, I focused on two areas: technology and the future leadership team. Technology was the first priority, and a realm in which we have made substantial strides. When I took over, we were using a dated computer program and still relying heavily on paper; some staff members still insisted they needed typewriters for certain functions. This was in 2010! It was clear to me this was an area that warranted real change. But you need to handle this sort of transition delicately—you don't want to upset the apple cart *too* much. My first project along these lines had a more modest goal: let's get all our shared resources in one place.

At this point, we depended on physical filing cabinets—meaning that paperwork would pile up until someone got to it. Technicians had files stuck in the seat cushions of their trucks. Files were removed and never put back. While my staff still sometimes laments the "glory days" of paper, I think they forget that pulling a file sometimes took minutes—or even hours—and now it only takes a few clicks of a button.

> During those first five years, I focused on two areas: technology and the future leadership team.

The new filing structure allowed for clearer file searches. We established protocols for scanning our "heritage" paper files, and we back-scanned seven years' worth of paper. At the end of this process, we ceremoniously threw the filing cabinets off the loading dock.

The other major technological change involved our software system. It was antiquated, looking like the interface to an Atari video game, going the way of the dinosaurs. I knew we needed to replace it, because it was the foundation of our payroll, customer database, entire accounting package, and inventory. It touched every pivotal piece of our business. We spent a year looking for a replacement system and another preparing the transition—then another year (or more) getting staff comfortable with the new system.

That system, which we so painstakingly learned and adapted to, is now vital to running our organization. We're more mobile friendly and almost 100 percent paperless, living in a much different world from 2010.

The other focus was the current leadership team and succession plans. Many of our core staff were nearing retirement age, with no replacements in the wings. Others were in positions that didn't necessarily fit their skill set. And in some cases, a department was growing beyond what the manager was comfortable handling. This was a team of people who had done a wonderful job building the company over the previous decades. They had experience and knowledge that would be difficult to replace. But this was my father's leadership team, not mine.

Developing a succession plan involved asking myself whom I could lean on and trust—who had the potential for real leadership? I learned that training the future generation of leaders is not something that happens in a few months. It takes years. So, while it was a difficult conversation, I had to encourage the current team to look a few years out and help me find and develop the future team.

I knew it would be years before these individuals, once identified, were put into their leadership roles. We spent that time training and preparing them. They were assigned to executive leadership boards, worked with business coaches, and spent many days in soft-skills training.

> **Training the future generation of leaders is not something that happens in a few months. It takes years.**

The most impactful training I could offer these future leaders, by far, was to involve them in the management of a department or the company. I would copy them on conversations, share outcomes with them, and discuss how we could have handled things better. It was important to help them accrue experience before they took on their new roles; good leaders draw on information from their own backgrounds to handle challenges.

After years of planning and training, we have now transitioned all of these individual positions. I was able to restructure the company organization to better suit future growth. This process was a necessity. There were so many managers that I simply couldn't support them all effectively; I was stretched too thin. Having a team of thoroughly trained leaders in place allowed me to maximize my time and also lend needed support to employees in various fields company-wide.

I'm very happy with the changes. They have been critical in getting Fireline to the point we're at today, which is now a company with more than two hundred employees and pushing $30 million in sales—and poised to continue growing. Incorporating those changes wasn't easy.

I am often asked how I made it through those first few years, how people received me as a leader. Looking back, I realize I used certain aspects of my personality to my advantage in the business world. I love strategy. I thrive on collaborating with a team, fixing a problem, seeing progress.

Building a successful organization requires an innovative mind-set. And while I do love to analyze that progress with a good spreadsheet, I don't want to live in one. I need others to help me build my ideas into reality. It takes a team of people with strengths that balance out my own.

I quickly learned that when entering a meeting with a customer. As a woman, it was just assumed that I was the "sales girl." People would talk around me as if I were not in the room. But when I approached the situation with an air of confidence, that changed. I'd sit down, put my hands out to my sides, and take a position of power. Using words, tone, and body language, I showed I was the one in charge—and found that people respond to confidence. They respond to strength. From that point onward, my age and gender no longer mattered.

I had the good fortune to go to an all-girls high school. I grew up in a world without sexism. The all-girls environment was conducive to developing strong female personalities. I, therefore, entered the workforce quite oblivious to the idea that women were expected to be demure. I'm sure I surprised more than a few people when I sat down at the table and simply took the lead.

My experience can apply to anyone suddenly faced with a business leadership opportunity. Many people, but particularly women, have the tendency to not say yes to something unless they are 100 percent convinced they can do it. I'm a huge advocate of saying yes to opportunities and then getting to 100 percent.

When I entered this industry, I eagerly accepted the chance to sit on industry boards—even when it seemed I was the token female. I didn't care; these were opportunities to gain firsthand knowledge and add my voice to the conversation. I absorbed an incredible amount of industry knowledge just by sitting on these boards. I met leaders in my industry, gained their respect, and built a network of resources for my business. And, in many cases, I contributed more than I expected, making changes and taking the lead on projects that helped to grow those organizations. Had I turned down these opportunities for fear of not being qualified, I would have cheated myself of some valuable experiences.

While personal development and team development are important, there is no doubt that I would have been lost without a strong peer network supporting me. I would advise anyone who encounters unexpected leadership to seek out such a network among other leaders. I was fortunate to have two peer groups. One was in my industry, made up of other fire-protection business owners throughout the country. The other was a group of local business owners. These two groups allowed me to speak about the company's challenges and potential solutions in a candid way, with like-minded business people offering me support.

Even today, with my years of experience, my peer groups educate me, help me make decisions, and share their lessons. I get everything from legal advice to feedback on hiring decisions to experiences with implementing new software. Business owners who assume they know it all are kidding themselves. Every business leader struggles. Everyone needs help and advice, from the novice to the veteran. A peer group is vital to success.

While personal development and team development are important, there is no doubt that I would have been lost without a strong peer network supporting me.

As unexpected as my ascension into leadership was, I feel strongly it was the right move for me, the company, and my family. Even with all the challenges, I still get up every day excited to go to work. I remember that when I was growing up, my father would take my brother and me to the office so he could work on Saturdays. Who would want to work on the weekend? But I get it now. It's not just my work—it's an important aspect of my life. I get to provide jobs, contribute to my community, and build a legacy. Fireline has a long history—and now I'm a part it.

SEEING THE BIG PICTURE

MARK CISSELL, PRESIDENT AND
CEO, KATZABOSCH, P.A.

When I joined the accounting, auditing, and business consultation firm KatzAbosch in 1985, business was done much differently than it is today. Perhaps the biggest change affecting our practice—and most small to medium-sized businesses—is technology.

It wasn't until the late 1980s and early 1990s that we stopped preparing tax returns by hand. Today, high-speed technology is incorporated seamlessly into our practice processes and culture. If a client needs to make a correction to virtually any item, it can typically be done on the spot—by someone sitting at home in their bedroom, for example. He or she can resolve the issue or make the change and return the revised document to the client instantly.

As technology evolves, clients expect quick turnaround and almost immediate response to their questions. Keeping a finger on the pulse of industry technology allows our team to exceed those expectations. However, clients aren't the only ones whose expectations have been altered by a world of lightning-speed tech. Our firm's young employees also tend to have differing expectations from their predecessors.

Given the ease of operation in nearly every sector of business, younger employees often expect to work less. They are not lazy or uninterested by any means; they've simply adapted to an environment in which a great deal of once-difficult labor has been automated.

> *As technology evolves, clients expect quick turn-around and almost immediate response to their questions. Keeping a finger on the pulse of industry technology allows our team to exceed those expectations.*

Therefore, in addition to technological advancements, we see employee expectations as one of the primary shifts in KatzAbosch. Our ability to mentor employees and manage their expectations while remaining relevant and continuing to grow is paramount.

Mentoring staff allows us to ensure that one of the company's chief objectives remains in focus and practiced throughout the company; that is to *always* think like business people, not simply like accountants.

At the beginning of one's career, it's important to be a technician in a sense—to have a thorough comprehension of the niche industry one is serving and to understand the nuts and bolts, from compliance to troubleshooting. In other words, you must know the task at hand inside out.

However, it's just as important to grow beyond being simply a technician and become a trusted advisor. At KatzAbosch, this focus translates into consultation work that extends well beyond compliance to aspects such as auditing, accounting, and taxation. One of the hats I wear as CEO, president, and director is that of trainer—I lead employees to think constantly and consistently about this overriding question: "Where can we add value?"

In our practice's work with industries that range from construction and real estate to biotech, health, and life sciences, this attention to adding value manifests in numerous ways. Our team helps businesses spot and correct inefficiencies in day-to-day operations. We also frequently assist with staffing considerations, thereby helping our clients to make sure the right people are serving in the right roles.

Michael E. Gerber, author of *The E-Myth*, says, "Most entrepreneurs are merely technicians with an entrepreneurial seizure. Most entrepreneurs fail because you are working IN your business rather than ON your business."[1] While not all team members consider themselves entrepreneurs or aspire to that role, what Gerber says gets to the heart of what it means to think like a businessperson—to step back, assess where needs exist and how they can be answered, and focus on the forest rather than just the trees.

In small to medium-sized businesses, leaders frequently wear multiple hats. This can make it difficult to step back far enough from ongoing operations to truly see the broader picture. As experienced outsiders looking in, our team can more clearly assess a business in totality. This enables us to make specific recommendations to help our clients run their businesses more efficiently and profitably.

When I look at the elements that help our team operate at maximum efficiency, the one that constantly stands out is people. When you treat people on your team as a valuable resource—when you invest the time in not only training but also truly mentoring them—then you're really looking after your company's future. You're cultivating a team that operates as a cohesive unit, one that will thoroughly understand the company's philosophy.

---

1   Michael Gerber, The E-Myth (New York: Harper Business, 1986).

If you're the leader of a small or medium-sized business, building up your team members to embrace the broader facets of the job, as well as the technical aspects, also allows you to focus on those matters you and you alone can handle. Moreover, you're fostering competency and loyalty in your employees, thereby helping to ensure you'll have a long-lasting team that you can count on.

> **When I look at the elements that help our team operate at maximum efficiency, the one that constantly stands out is people.**

Some important lessons offered to those I mentor are business-related in a traditional sense. Others are less so. As useful as it is to train strict technicians to think like businesspeople, you sometimes have to nudge the business-minded to think like people whose lives include work ... but are not limited to it.

Along those lines, some of the same skills that make for a successful and happy life outside the office will improve your performance within it. For instance, if you want to keep improving, then remain open to the opinions of others. If you want to build and maintain strong ties—at home, at work, or wherever you are—then try not to react to things immediately. Learn to put a pin in a discussion when necessary—so you can truly process the matter at hand and think through reactions other than the first one that occurs to you.

I encourage those I mentor to remember that life is short. When we get caught up in daily worries, we tend to convince ourselves that every molehill is a mountain in disguise, and then we're perpetually worried. Then we neglect our health—and we're no longer enjoying ourselves.

Health is foundational to our success in every arena of life, including business. Yet it's often one of the first areas we ignore. I encourage anyone whose main goal is professional success to reflect on their stress level, along with their tendency to indulge in negative thoughts and doomsday concerns.

My own years of experience have taught me that almost everything is fixable. The maxim "Don't sweat the small stuff" has long been popular for a reason. Most people who reach a point of prominence and seniority in business can look back on their formative work years and see the many ways in which their worries were needless. They can remember times when they became so stressed by a seemingly insurmountable problem that their health took a turn for the worse.

Here again, we get back to the notion of stepping back. When you're a business consultant, you have to step back to assess the whole picture before you can make recommendations for improvement. As an individual technician, businessperson, manager, or entrepreneur, you need to take the same sort of step back to assess the larger picture of yourself: your health, your stress level, your mind-set, your goals, and so on.

The people I train are always encouraged to be their very best, but I also like to remind them that there are some elements of success completely out of their hands. The part you own in the equation is being good at what you do, but when you've done your part, relax—you've done all you can do. Then sit back and enjoy your success.

PRODUCT KNOWLEDGE, LEADERSHIP, AND MARKETING: PERSPECTIVES FROM A FORMER NAVAL INTELLIGENCE OFFICER

CARL STROBEL, CHAIRMAN, FIBERPLUS

I always remember the old saying, "If you build a better mousetrap, the world will beat a path to your door." One day, while working in the field of computers and computer networks, I thought I had found that better mousetrap.

After I graduated from college, I embarked on a twenty-one-year career in the US Navy, where I worked in intelligence. The computer industry was just coming of age at that time, and I became enmeshed in it. I learned all about my field, which had become vital for handling the mass amount of data in the world of intelligence.

After retiring from the navy, I eventually found myself working for a contractor at a large Department of Defense agency that provided computer-related support. It struck me that some of the computer networks at that agency depended heavily on fiber-optic infrastructure. So I decided to use my technical expertise and start a company offering that.

Even though I had no business experience to my name, in 1992, I boldly launched my company, FiberPlus, Inc. We offered fiber-optic technology for networks. The advantages of speed and capacity in fiber-optic-based networks were overwhelming. Soon enough the world indeed came to my door.

For some months, my company was one of the very few that offered the significant upgrade that a fiber-optic infrastructure provided. Marketing consisted mostly of letting potential users know that my company existed. Things went swimmingly for a while. All types of consumers, not only commercial clients but also state and federal government agencies, were soon clamoring for this new technology. It was an exciting time to work in fiber optics.

Unfortunately for me, established network companies started moving into the field. They quickly became serious competitors. And they offered more network services than installation of fiber-optic cable.

At this point, my lack of prior business experience manifested itself in a negative way. My naval service had given me plenty of experience in directing people and setting and achieving goals, and I certainly knew the technology. But I knew nothing about sales or marketing. I didn't know how to pivot our products to truly distinguish us from our competitors.

I looked for an experienced outside perspective to help me. I needed to become as strong on the marketing side as I felt I was in leadership and the technical-knowledge side. For me, joining The Alternative Board (TAB) was key.

The TAB group that I became part of included ten small businesses CEOs. The constant and primary concern of most of them was marketing and sales. This was true for an accounting firm, a construction company, and a law firm, among others. The CEOs talked a great deal about ideas that had worked and ideas that hadn't. I learned a great deal listening to their discussions.

One of the most important things I learned was that I was not selling technology; I was selling a solution. Being a techie, I was excited primarily about the technology. But finally, it was driven home to me that our customers were not buying fiber-optic technology for its own sake. They were buying a way to improve their operations.

What I learned is that after you've built this more impressive product, you need to be able to meet the demands of the customers who are attracted to it. I did this by focusing on product knowledge and marketing efforts. Even more so, I applied to the world of fiber optics the leadership lessons I'd picked up from my previous life in the navy.

The technology we were using made significant improvements possible in the usefulness of networked computer systems. Fiber

> *One of the most important things I learned was that I was not selling technology; I was selling a solution.*

gave us additional bandwidth and interoperability, but one persistent problem was that of security.

In the old days of physical security and video surveillance, for instance, you'd have somebody sitting at a desk with maybe ten or twelve different surveillance cameras feeding images to a monitor. An individual would be, at all hours of the day and night, watching these monitors. If they saw something suspicious, they'd call up the security division. But you have to wonder how much attention they were really paying at two o'clock in the morning. That, in a nutshell, was the old way.

Today, networks have been developed to the point that videos are passed on a fiber-optic network directly to computers programmed to look for specific parameters. Security personnel can be alerted specifically if a problem is detected, such as someone trying to get through a fence late at night. It can not only specify the location but can also determine whether the activity is benign—a bird or a squirrel, for example, hitting the fence. This prevents many false alarms.

Another example is the burgeoning field of facial recognition. Instead of relying on a person to swipe a magnetic card or enter a code at a locked door, a fiber-optic-based network can note the person's facial characteristics and send them to a computer database where they are compared with the images of those with authorized access. No worry about an access card being loaned to someone or an access code being shared.

With use of computer networks expanding rapidly, we had opportunities to do more than install the infrastructure. For example, we discovered demand for the installation of total video surveillance and inventory control systems, not just the infrastructure to support them.

We beefed up our technical capabilities, our marketing efforts, and our sales department to keep pace with the advances of technology. When it came to technology, we made it clear to consumers that we cared about improving the old—as well as ushering in something new. For example, in addition to our fiber-optic products, we provided computer and network technology in areas where high-speed copper cables were adequate.

Today, networks are used in ways we couldn't have imagined when I founded my company. Many teachers are now illustrating their lessons with material that students see on a video display in the classroom. Some restaurant chains have put simple computers at tables, allowing customers to review the menu and order their meal—and play computer games while they wait. In short, there's hardly any area of modern life that doesn't rely to some degree on computer networks. It's imperative that we keep abreast of not only new technology but also the new markets that spring up.

An important element of our business development strategy was our sales force. Initially, we allied ourselves as subcontractors with large businesses and with the federal government, as these were the institutions best positioned to adopt fiber optics. But clearly we couldn't stop there. We recruited an excellent sales force and sales leadership to knock on the right doors—schools, for instance. We developed relationships with several local school districts and community colleges, helping them use information technology to support their missions.

On the marketing side, we also hosted the occasional seminar to introduce a new technology, or a new twist on an existing one. Overall, we've approached marketing from the standpoint of getting the word out about not only our newest technology, but also our experience—what major projects we've worked on in the past that might interest potential new clients.

However, one of the most important steps I took regarding marketing—and every other aspect of the business—involved hiring some very sharp people as the company grew. I'm a believer that you hire people with impressive business acumen and shrewd minds; then you listen to them. And that's what I did. When a problem arose, I'd get a group of us together to talk about how best to solve it. We would then proceed from there.

This touches on another important quality I consider necessary for any business leader to cultivate—leadership. Even if you have inside-out knowledge of your product or service—and you've learned the ropes of marketing—you still need to direct and inspire your people.

After a twenty-year military career followed by an even longer tenure leading FiberPlus, I've come to the conclusion that civilians have a misconception about the military—that you give an order and people jump to it. That they have to just do it or they're in deep trouble. This is not true. The navy is actually similar to many businesses and any other team-based organization, in that you have to get people inspired.

However, one of the most important steps I took regarding marketing—and every other aspect of the business—involved hiring some very sharp people as the company grew.

Imagine a sailor assigned to a ship about to be deployed from the Pacific Coast to the Far East. He's a young guy, his wife has just had a baby, and he has to tell her, "I'll see you and the baby in five or six months." What are the chances you'll get great work from him? This is someone who's likely to do the minimum required—unless you can inspire some enthusiasm in him.

One of my own inspirations is a quotation from Napoleon Bonaparte. After a group of his troops marched by in formation, Napoleon turned to one of his civilian ministers and asked what he thought. The minister replied that it was all very nice, but he wondered about the silly little pieces of colored ribbon the soldiers wore on their tunics. What in the world was that about?

Napoleon replied, "Men will risk their lives, even die, for those ribbons."

I've always kept this in mind. I served in and around Vietnam for nearly three and a half years early in the war, first at sea and then in the air. I found that many people—including me—would take all kinds of risks and afterward take immense pride in the medals earned. In business, as in the military, it's often about being acknowledged for one's efforts.

One of the specific tools of inspiration and acknowledgement I brought from my navy experience was something called Bravo Zulu. In the old days, before you could communicate between ships by radio, they used signal flags. The signal flags B (Bravo) and Z (Zulu) flown together meant "well done." To see this praise coming from the admiral's flagship meant a great deal for those receiving it.

In the workplace, I implemented the practice of giving Bravo Zulu awards. It was a chart with the Bravo Zulu flags, beneath which were the names of the people being recognized and what it was they'd accomplished. I put this on the wall for everyone to see.

Another leadership lesson involved visiting the troops. At FiberPlus, much of our work takes place outside the office, the bulk involving sending crews out into the field. So I started going out to these work sites in order to show our team that I was interested in what they were doing—and to talk to them about their work. I would frequently take along someone from the desk-bound office staff so they, too, could better understand what our teams were doing—and enduring—in the field.

One of the primary ways to make your employees feel genuinely valued is also every bit as valuable to me as it is to them: asking their advice. Are we doing this the right way? What do you think we should be doing?

When you acknowledge employees, though, keep in mind that you can't offer phony congratulations. They'll detect it if you're just blowing smoke; your appreciation must be real. One of the primary ways to make them feel genuinely valued is also every bit as valuable to me as it is to them: asking their advice. Are we doing this the right way? What do you think we should be doing?

I remember when the business was maybe two or three years old. One of the employees said, "Carl, we know it's your company, but you make us feel like we're part owners too." That's one of the best compliments I've ever received.

I take guidance in this matter from an admiral—one of the finest—whom I worked for on the aircraft carrier *USS Midway*. We were off the Gulf of Tonkin conducting air strikes against North Vietnam.

This admiral oversaw a group of captains, commanders, and junior officers like me. But he didn't command. He didn't say, "Do this." He requested our opinions. And he was so pleasant and nice and truly interested in getting the job done right that we all worked as hard as we could. We would willingly put in long hours under very difficult conditions because we didn't want to see him fail. We wanted the commander of the Pacific Fleet to think he was as good as we thought he was. It was one of the clearest lessons I have experienced in how to motivate people: Talk to them. Don't be arbitrary or authoritative. Work with them and solicit their thoughts. Ask them to do the things that are needed. Don't imply "Do this or else."

On the strategic side, one valuable leadership lesson I've adopted represents something of a deviation from my days in the navy. During my service, my division was not closely monitored. We had general goals to achieve but were also tasked, as each occasion arose, with figuring out the best way to meet them under existing circumstances. In essence, we were in a reactive mode, facing a changing environment.

Through my own experiences consulting with other business leaders and my association with TAB, I've learned the importance of having a written strategic plan for a business. It should contain not only goals over a five- to ten-year period but also deadlines for the steps required toward those goals. For instance, if you're going to adopt and sell a new technology, establish deadlines for getting people trained. Then designate a specific date for beginning to advertise, and so on.

By integrating and applying lessons from my days in the navy with what I learned from strategic partnerships along the way, I've watched FiberPlus grow far beyond my initial expectations.

We started off with just an office manager, four or five technicians, and me. As the demand for fiber-optic technology and computer networking grew, we eventually branched out into three separate companies: FiberPlus, FiberPlus Federal Systems, and Pennsylvania Networks.

These three companies now compose a network of more than 250 employees, with offices in Maryland, Pennsylvania, Virginia, and Ohio. By focusing on a combination of evolving technical knowledge, leadership, and marketing, we've been able to ensure that FiberPlus experiences growth while staying relevant and competitive—and that it remains a successful workplace that our team members can be proud of.

THE PRICE OF YES: HOW NEVER SAYING NO CAN BE THE RIGHT STRATEGY

JAMES DEGRAFFENREID, CHAIRMAN, EEI COMMUNICATIONS AND TAB FACILITATOR

I was relaxing on the patio behind my house one day almost two decades ago, overlooking the beautiful river and the forest on the opposite side. My daughter interrupted my reverie to tell me that a man was at the front door asking to see me. I wasn't exactly excited about the interruption, but I headed through the house to see who was looking for me. I never imagined that this encounter would inspire an idea that would serve me well through the rest of my business career.

At my door I met a pleasant, fortyish man with intelligent eyes and a ready smile. After politely begging my forgiveness for imposing on my privacy, he launched into his story. He had grown up locally but had moved to the West Coast some years before to be part of the management team growing an early dot-com. He explained they had started with angel investment, achieved early success, taken on some major venture-capital funding—and hit the long ball. Not long after, a large company acquired them. My newfound acquaintance had found himself a modestly wealthy man.

I found his story fascinating, and we spoke for some time about his experience. About how he had learned to manage growth. About balance—being aggressive enough to maximize growth without becoming too aggressive and getting too far out in front of his emerging market space. About the strange venture-capital world of the time, so mesmerized by notions of establishing early market dominance that the result was more attention paid to how much could be lost buying market share than to profitability.

Finally, we got around to the reason for his presence on my doorstep. He told me that, having enough money to live anywhere he wanted, he had decided to move back to where he had grown up. Specifically, my neighborhood, since it was "on the water" and was where he had always wanted to live. I readily agreed it was a truly great place to live. But what did I have to do with his plans?

He was direct—he wanted to buy my house.

Actually, he was canvassing the neighborhood looking for anyone willing to sell. He wanted to get around real estate agent fees. He said my house was one of his favorites.

I told him I was flattered—and agreed with his judgment about my house—but there was no way I would sell it. Indeed, it was one of the best homes in our wonderful neighborhood. But with my kids in the middle of their adolescence and established at school, we just weren't in the market. I wished him good luck and told him I hoped we would become neighbors. After a few more pleasantries, he left and knocked on my neighbor's door.

Later that afternoon I described the offer to my wife. She hadn't been home when this fellow came knocking. She asked a perfectly natural question that hadn't occurred to me—how much was he willing to pay?

Sheepishly, I had to admit that I hadn't inquired. I had been so focused on "not being in the market" that I never considered price.

And then a big question popped into my head: Was I really not willing to sell my house? Or might there have been a number that would have moved me to consider a different answer?

Was there, in other words, a *price of yes*?

I pondered this issue. Clearly, we loved our home. But there were other lovely homes around us that

> *I had been so focused on "not being in the market" that I never considered price.*

might have been for sale. We were on the water, but so were other homes—some of them in the same school district. So, could we have entertained an offer? *Should* we have entertained an offer?

After some consideration, I came to the conclusion that there was a price at which we could have sold, found a comparable home, made up for the inconvenience and expense of moving, and still put some extra cash in the bank. Clearly there was a price—the price of yes—that would have made selling a good deal for us.

But could we have gotten a price that made the sale *right* for us?

On further thought, it occurred to me that the decision really wasn't up to us. Our "price of yes" was what we needed to make a deal. The question of whether it was acceptable to the buyer, or not, was up to the buyer. Only he could make that decision.

But we didn't let him make that decision. I said no *for* him. He never got the chance to ponder whether our price was right for him.

Thinking about this took me back to my early business career, when I was starting up the ladder at a large corporation. I was given an assignment in our sales department—what today we call "business development." I arrived for an appointment with a potential customer whose quarters were dilapidated. Based on the look of the place, I wondered if this outfit could ever spend the money to buy my product. Sitting there, I came very close to not making the call.

I almost "said no for the customer," but I followed through with the appointment and the prospect became a customer. Many times in my future business career, in both application and education, I profited from not saying no for the customer.

Yet, in my private life, I'd ignored two rules that I'd come to consider absolutes in my business career. First, never say no for the customer; second, always consider the price of yes.

I also learned that these two principles applied not only to the negotiation phase of business development, but also to a host of other business disciplines. For example, in product development, I came to realize that internally focused beliefs about customer needs and desires were often erroneous—and could lead to disastrous decisions. In a way, developing products from unverified opinions about the customer's needs and desires is saying no for the customer and ignoring the price of yes.

Without proper customer research and test marketing, it can be easy to miss features the customer is looking for or include features they don't want and wouldn't pay for. To get product design right, you need to know what the customer wants and what they are willing to pay for—what their price of yes is.

Later in my career I became heavily involved in mergers and acquisitions, finding the price of yes to be strategically valuable there as well. While there are numerous objective financial procedures for valuing company worth, the final price often turns on one party's price of yes.

This is often true in "strategic purchases." The target company represents nonfinancial valuable market position and/or synergies that are capable of bringing earnings multiples well above what traditional financial analysis produces. The difference in winning or losing in a competitive acquisition environment often depends on a keen understanding of the target's price of yes.

So, the next time you find yourself saying, "Ah, that customer will never buy this," think again. Check your assumptions, make sure your offering is sound, and then let the customer say yes or no.

If you're tempted to reflexively say no to an offer, stop yourself, think hard about it, and offer your price of yes.

And what about the potential buyer who showed up at my doorstep that day? Well, he bought a lovely home down the street for 30 percent over market value. He really wanted a home in that neighborhood—and for him it was worth the over-market value price. So he "won," as did the seller who didn't say no and instead asked for his price of yes—and got it.

If you're tempted to reflexively say no to an offer, stop yourself, think hard about it, and offer your price of yes.

UNLOCKING YOUR POTENTIAL: LESSONS FROM A BUSINESS COACH

SUSAN KATZ, CEO, THE KATZ ADVANTAGE AND TAB FACILITATOR

When most people think of publishing, they think of writing and editing—but the business side is critical as well. For twenty of the nearly thirty years I spent in higher education publishing, I served in an executive management role—running profit-and-loss centers. Working within the various divisions of a broader publishing institution helped me gain an understanding of small business operation, while still benefiting from the safety net of a larger business.

I left publishing when I realized that I was not going to be the person to bring us into the digital age. I learned the vast importance of recognizing when you are no longer in alignment with the work you're doing. It was fortuitous that around the same time that I was thinking of leaving, I got laid off; that opened the door for me to start my own business, which focused on executive coaching, leadership development, and facilitation.

In my present business, I work with many company owners and key executives affiliated with everything from very small businesses to large organizations. And though this clearly represents a broad range of clients, the principle behind coaching is the same: It's all about people and human behavior. My primary focus is helping people understand their own behavior and, thereby, improve the way they work. I help them become more effective and productive, as well as better aligned with and fulfilled by their work.

I teach business owners to focus on building a business that can eventually be sold. It's an asset, and they should continually make efforts to expand the value of it. A critical—and frequently overlooked—piece of that puzzle is that owners must figure out how their own skill sets and goals can best align with the business.

> **My primary focus is helping people understand their own behavior and, thereby, improve the way they work.**

While they're on that journey—aligning themselves with what they're best at—they should be finding other people to do the rest of the necessary work. Most of them start out working many different jobs within their company, and then, as the business grows, they reach a point when they find themselves working 24/7. As difficult as it may be, they have to start hiring people and letting go of some of the work. As a business owner, your role is to create jobs—not to work jobs.

This can be a painful process. I've seen many business owners who hired the wrong people and ended up feeling burned, very hesitant to hire again. They began to believe that they would never find the right individuals. But hiring people you trust to do the work is key to growing an organization.

In addition to hiring the right people for business growth, it's important for business owners to better target their efforts. Entrepreneurs often feel they must be all things to all people; they fear that narrowing their focus will mean ruling out potential customers. However, the reverse is usually true. The more you narrow your focus, the easier it is for people to understand what you do. Once you're working with a client on one service, you can naturally introduce the idea that you could also handle a related service. Starting out with a honed focus is the best way to get in the door with clients and then receive referrals to other related businesses.

The issue of focus extends well beyond the realm of sales and marketing. People who start businesses tend to have lots of ideas—and can end up chasing so many rabbits that it becomes difficult to catch any one of them. Getting clear about your direction and then creating a manageable action plan will help ensure that your best, most viable opportunities don't slip away.

Another challenge I've seen that impacts nearly all companies—of any size, in any industry—is communication. This comes down to self-awareness, of being cognizant of how you impact the people in your organization. Business leaders who demonstrate self-awareness have an easier time fostering effective communication among their employees.

Getting clear about your direction and then creating a manageable action plan will help ensure that your best, most viable opportunities don't slip away.

Organizations experience greatly improved communications when adopting a policy of treating one another like customers. Sometimes people in organizations get very comfortable with one another; they even end up treating one another like family. When interacting with customers, though, employees interact differently by putting their best foot forward, being willing to answer any questions, and showing an interest in dealing with customer objections. Employees' relationships with one another would be improved if their communication were based on these same principles.

It's the business owner's responsibility to communicate—clearly and directly—what is expected of the employees. This needs to take into account both performance and behavioral expectations. Doing so helps establish effective communication within the organization.

Speaking of which, before you can tell your employees what you expect of them, you need a firm grasp on what you want the business culture to look like. Naturally, it will evolve over time, but it's still important to start with a focused vision.

This need to understand and communicate company culture is exemplified in an experience of one of my clients. The company has a small staff—eight people in all—and they're all very collegial with one another. The culture is one of openness, honesty, and independence. Staff members are motivated to drive their own successes and handle their own responsibilities without coaxing.

But they hired someone who didn't really fit that profile. While he was a great employee in many ways, he needed a lot more hand-holding. Because the company wanted to give him every opportunity to succeed, feedback became critical. They made it a point to have regular conversations in which they provided direction and shared concrete expectations with him.

This company's experience provides a good example of how to handle an employee who doesn't fit into the organization. Your first step is to help that employee, setting clear expectations with regard to behavior and company culture. This may be enough—the individual in question may adapt to those standards and come to fit seamlessly into your company culture. On the other hand, you may eventually see that the person is not a good match.

Regardless of how a new employee fits, ongoing employee feedback is critical to success. You need to let your employees know what it is they're doing that is in alignment with expectations—*and* where they need to improve (while providing the support to help them succeed).

Rather than providing feedback, many inexperienced managers will let mistakes accumulate. Once that happens, any conversation is going to be more difficult. When you establish a habit of frequently providing positive, constructive feedback, the process will get easier with every conversation.

A well-oiled feedback loop also encourages accountability. Employees who are given boundaries, direction, and leadership are apt to hold themselves responsible for their own performance and success. To support that process, use phrases such as these:

"Help me understand what's happening."

"This is what I'm observing."

"We talked about this—where is the disconnect?"

"What's keeping you from doing what we talked about?"

By giving evaluative feedback of this nature, you not only promote accountability, but also feed into the central needs of most employees for autonomy, mastery, and purpose, which nearly everyone wants.

> *A well-oiled feedback loop also encourages accountability. Employees who are given boundaries, direction, and leadership are apt to hold themselves responsible for their own performance and success.*

Millennials tend to be especially purpose driven, and they, in particular, are likely to appreciate the ongoing feedback.

Make sure that feedback doesn't become a process in which you point out flaws and needs but never follow through with a plan. Even though employees do desire autonomy, they also rely heavily on their leaders' guidance. One of the best ways to cultivate an environment of progress and improvement is to incorporate regular training for your employees.

Organizations such as Gallup have shown that employee engagement drives all business results, and employee engagement is driven by employees' relationships with their managers and peer groups.[2] And what drives those relationships is the type of conversations employees have with each other. If you coach and engage your employees on a routine basis, you will gain a better understanding of what's important to them. They will feel more valued, which will lead to greater engagement and, ultimately, better results.

The business owner's job is to provide vision, strategy, direction, and coaching to their employees. Hire the right people and then, rather than working all the jobs, work with your employees to help them do their jobs more successfully.

And finally, the most successful leaders with whom I work utilize outside resources to help develop themselves. These may be advisory boards, mentors, or coaches. High performers in sports use coaches—so do the most successful business people. The right coach serves as a sounding board and will help you gain clarity about the beliefs getting in your way—helping you to discover new ways to

---

2   Susan Sorenson, "How Employee Engagement Drives Growth," Gallup, June 20, 2013, https://www.gallup.com/workplace/236927/employee-engagement-drives-growth.aspx.

think and eventually to do things that will unlock your potential in business.

SHINING FROM THE INSIDE OUT: GREAT COMPANY CULTURE ATTRACTS GREAT EMPLOYEES

CAROLINE KIRSCHNICK, PRESIDENT, EMR

When I joined The Electric Motor Repair Company (EMR) in 2003, there was still what I'd call an old-school management mentality. While the company had always been family oriented and made treating its workforce well a priority, employees were employees—and managers were managers. The line was clearly drawn. But I had a very different vision for the company—one that allowed for a greater degree of collaboration and community across all facets of the organization.

Essentially, I grew up through the company. In doing so, I made it my mission to foster a more dynamic culture, one in which you were not just invited to contribute but truly felt safe and valued in your contributions. This encouraged staff to not only get involved, but stay involved—and make this story *their* story—and, ultimately, to realize success both professionally and personally. Part of this mission was to create the sense that every EMR employee is part of one big family. EMR is the Kauffman family's business, but each employee is an EMR family member.

One important thing I realized early on is that as a business leader, your most valuable resource is your people. They are working for the company, doing their jobs, day in and day out. They know the business better than anyone. Who better to solicit ideas and input from than the people who are out there on the front line? I saw endless potential in so many people. It just needed to be unleashed. I waited, sometimes impatiently, for the day that I could tap into the knowledge and talent we had right under our noses.

EMR is a service business, tracing its history back to 1927. It has been in my family for three genera-

> *As a business leader, your most valuable resource is your people.*

tions, passing from my grandfather to my father to me. I have a sister and three brothers, one older than I am. When we were growing up, my father often tried to spark his interest in the business. I needed no such encouragement.

Even as a young child, before I truly understood the world, I would make declarations like, "I want to be in the business!" I used to "play office," pretending to take orders and keep paperwork filed and organized. I couldn't yet comprehend the nuances of the family business, but I knew it was very special that we had one—and my passion developed from that point.

Naturally, passion is an important element of any successful business venture. While I was proud of the family business, I also wanted to make certain I wasn't neglecting other potential passions. At various junctures, I entertained the idea of studying both sociology and nursing. When I finished my undergraduate education, after having settled on a degree in public relations, I realized there was nothing I'd rather do than work for EMR.

While our company's core competencies have remained steady through the years, our specific focus has certainly evolved. At one time, the motor shop—where industrial motor pumps and drives were repaired and rewound—represented the bulk of our business. It is still an aspect of EMR, but now accounts for 15 to 20 percent of the business. Presently, we primarily focus on the commercial-kitchen industry. We install, fix, and perform preventative maintenance on any piece of equipment you'd find in a professional kitchen. Our customers range from restaurants and fast food establishments to institutions, such as schools, hospitals, and prisons.

In our industry, and any other industry that relies on highly skilled tradespeople and customer service, the *right* talent is hard to come by. In today's world, it sometimes seems that emotional intelligence, common sense, communication skills, and professionalism are in short supply. And in even shorter supply are young people who are learning the trades. Everyone, it seems, is fishing in the same shrinking pool of talent and excellence.

Any organization that employs top-of-the-line people will have a competitive edge. And I believe with all my heart that the way you attract and retain these qualified individuals is to shine from the inside out. Pay attention to company culture—it's the soul of your organization.

If you create a positive culture of collaboration, safety, certainty, communication, transparency, love, and connection, then you begin to shine from the inside out. In this kind of culture, employees find fulfillment in their work because

> *Any organization that employs top-of-the-line people will have a competitive edge.*

you have created an environment where they are an integral part of a bigger picture—the success of the organization. And people *want* that feeling, of being part of something bigger than themselves. They need to feel important. They need human connection. If you can provide this for people in the context of their work environment— where they spend a huge amount of their lives—then you will reap tremendous benefits.

Being focused on and dedicated to company culture can solve the employment gap that we tend to see in many industries, particularly blue-collar trades where there are more jobs than people qualified to do them. It can also help you in the never-ending fight to earn and keep your customer market share.

When you foster respect and care among your staff, they are much more likely to treat your customers in the same manner. Model the behavior you want from your people; the chance you'll receive it in return grows exponentially. My company's goal is to create a culture that EMR family members want to uphold, one that ensures that our culture will be shared with our customers.

Being successful in this way gives us an advantage over competitors who don't place as much importance on customer service—or understand how to instill these values in their staff. The basis of EMR's customer service is built on creating a feeling, an emotion, a positive and safe experience that is founded on trust.

A customer who feels safe with your company will be loyal to you and the services you provide them. Yes, you have to be technically capable and competent, but the feeling you create with your customers is of even greater importance. Humans thrive on connection, certainty, and safety. Fostering these elements within your organization is the key to success.

This is the central matter I dedicated myself to after joining EMR in 2003—empowering our employees to, in turn, empower our customers through their focus on positive company culture.

Naturally, you can't overhaul a company's culture overnight. For us, the shift happened gradually. It was amazing to watch. At first, employees were hesitant—not yet ready to accept that the new leadership was different, that things across the company were different, and that we were asking *them* to be different. However, we were consistent in our efforts to implement this cultural shift. It began to pay off: feeling comfortable and safe, the employees began to contribute excellent ideas.

We took specific steps to implement a more collaborative culture. We formed a group of thirty employees that cut across various positions and branches, tasking them with creating a system of values that answered this question: "As a company, how do we want to treat one another, and how do we want to treat our customers?"

Answering that question led us to author both a code of conduct and a customer service pledge. With these two documents in hand, we asked ourselves, what should we do with them? What comes next? We could certainly hang them on the wall—but then what? How should we go about infusing these ideas into our culture? How do we institute such far-reaching change?

From this line of questioning arose the Eye Spy program. Using software called Survey Square, this program encourages EMR family members to "spy" on one another, reporting outstanding work or behavior throughout the workday that exemplifies the values outlined in the code and pledge.

At the end of every month we do a random drawing from the names of all those who have participated—anyone who submitted a "spy" or was spied on—and we give out prizes. We even created a giant game board so people whose names are drawn can play Plinko in order to find out what their prize will be. This monthly process is captured on video and shared company-wide via email, social media, and our website.

Explaining our culture and this program is a major part of both our hiring and our onboarding process. Every employee is asked to commit to the code and the pledge. On their first day of orientation, new employees sign the code and pledge, which will hang on the wall in our corporate office. The documents look like the Declaration of Independence because, for us, it is our Declaration of Culture.

When we make hiring decisions, a potential employee's fit with this culture is a major deciding factor. We have woven it into performance reviews and discuss it in meetings, including it in both our reward and disciplinary actions.

We've extended this program of positivity to our customers and vendors as well. After explaining how Eye Spy works, we invite them to spy on our technicians and office staff, reporting when they see or hear us doing something exceptional—exceeding their expectations.

Another practice I implemented to help EMR adopt a positive company culture was consulting employees about any major business decision or potential change. Take our technicians' uniforms, for instance. When we began buying uniforms—instead of renting—we had the opportunity to overhaul our look. I consulted the technicians about everything. What style did they like? What color did they prefer? During the process, they knew their voices were being heard. And afterward, they could feel a sense of ownership in what they wore.

Obviously, there are decisions that must be made by top executives. But I work to put just as many as possible in the hands of our staff. I seek input through these group decisions and employee satisfaction surveys. I pursue every opportunity to acquire meaningful feedback.

As I said, whatever attitudes and practices we foster among employees, we extend to our customer base as well—and this certainly applies when it comes to feedback. In addition to conducting employee satisfaction surveys, we also place calls to customers to garner feedback. We ask them, "What could we have done better?" and, "What would you like to see us do more of?"

We also benefit from a founding membership we hold with an industry association of fellow service companies. The data collected by the association matches our own—with one specific point coming up over and over again. Customers always seem to ask for the same thing: better communication. This desire is universal among customers, and if you nail it, then your satisfaction rating among clients goes through the roof.

While feedback is useful, it can end up having an adverse effect if you don't use that information wisely. After we've asked the questions and received the answers, we take the next step—coming up with a solution to make things better. This is an area we've truly improved on with our customers, communicating to them, "We hear you, and we're taking these steps to give you what you need."

> While feedback is useful, it can end up having an adverse effect if you don't use that information wisely.

To enhance our discourse with customers, we've created positions within the company dedicated solely to proactive communication. For example, when we go on a service call and have to order parts, there's a person on our team who receives notification that we've placed an order. They reach out to the customer, letting them know their parts have been ordered, what type of shipping options were selected, and the approximate number of days before they can expect the parts. We are proactive.

Even in less-direct ways, the intense focus we place on communication trickles down to our customers. Because we believe in a communicative workplace, we frequently discuss our principles and the importance of strong communication. This infuses that focus into company culture, and thus into our full workforce, including our technicians.

Our technicians are EMR's eyes and ears—they represent the company to our customers on the front lines. When they leave our brick-and-mortar branches they are permeated with the concept of proactive communication. That value follows them to individual job sites. When they are with our customers, they communicate effectively and make our customers' experiences positive.

One of the most important elements of success—at an individual or a company level—is human connection. Everyone wants that connection. Everyone wants to be heard, to be understood, and to feel they can rely on one another. The more you deliver that to your employees, the more they, in turn, will deliver it to your customers.

Whatever service or product your company specializes in, your company is, at its core, *about* people. Once you understand that, then you can offer the human connection that your executives, employees, and customers all need.

Your company will have a culture whether you create one proactively or it creates itself. Don't leave something so influential up to chance. Be intentional. Create a culture where people thrive and shine, one of positivity and transparency for all.

POWERFUL WOMEN SPEAK

DENISE O'NEILL, PRESIDENT, TAB-BWI

The numerous charges of sexual harassment that began with the accusations against Harvey Weinstein in October 2017 expanded virally to include many others in the movie, media, and restaurant industries. Even politicians were involved in allegations of improper conduct with female employees. This all gave birth to the #MeToo movement, which called attention to the many women who have experienced sexual harassment in the workplace.

Sexual harassment highlights the broader issue of power dynamics that can affect women and men on the job. Powerful Women Speak addresses matters related to power—specifically how a large number of women inadvertently engage in what are considered low-power communication behaviors—and shares ideas on how they can more skillfully communicate in the work environment.

This is a highly relevant subject. The majority of women work, and according to a 2017 poll by MSN, more than 45 percent of women report being sexually harassed at work.[3] If you apply that

---

3   Rachel Gillett, "Sexual harassment isn't a Hollywood, tech, or media issue — it affects everyone," Business Insider, November 30, 2017, https://www.businessinsider.com/sexual-harassment-affects-nearly-everyone-2017-11.

figure to the population of women working in the United States today, that means somewhere in the neighborhood of 33 million women have experienced sexual harassment. That same poll reported about 15 percent of men had experienced sexual harassment.

The pervasive nature of sexual harassment hinders any company's ability to create an effective workplace, one in which people can commit their energies to doing their best work. Over the past twenty years, the norm has been to handle this by offering sexual harassment prevention training in the workplace. But the fact is that these training programs aren't working; a substantial body of research says that what you learn there may stick with you for three weeks—and then be forgotten.[4] So, what new approach might be taken to improve the current sexual harassment training programs?

> **Women and men communicate differently—which can be seen in verbal and nonverbal communication patterns.**

It starts with recognizing that women and men communicate differently—which can be seen in verbal and nonverbal communication patterns.[5] Current sexual harassment prevention training can be augmented with training programs focusing on developing skills that women can use to communicate more powerfully in the workplace.

About two decades ago, a linguist named Deborah Tannen first realized that when men and women communicated, it seemed as though they were doing so from different cultures—or even alterna-

---

4 "Ebbinghaus Forgetting Curve," Pscyhestudy, https://www.psychestudy.com/cognitive/memory/ebbinghaus-forgetting-curve.

5 Shari Kendall and Deborah Tannen, "Discourse and Gender," in *The Handbook of Discourse Analysis*, ed. by Deborah Schiffrin, Deborah Tannen, and Heidi E. Hamilton, (Oxford: Blackwell, 2001), 548-567.

tive worlds.[6] These differences, she found, encompass both verbal and nonverbal communication. Women tend to have higher levels of nonverbal communication than do men, and there are physiological reasons for that. Women have about 11 percent more neurons in the areas of the brain responsible for language and hearing. In women, the hippocampus—the center for memory and emotion—is larger than it is in men.

It makes sense, then, that women have an aptitude for being more verbally agile, for connecting better through friendships. Women have a demonstrable ability to read the emotions behind facial expressions and the tone of voice of someone they're speaking with. This ability is the backbone of a woman's intuition, a strength that allows women to unconsciously and intuitively read situations.

Women tend to engage in much more direct eye contact, smile more, and use bigger gestures when speaking.[7] Men, by comparison, tend to communicate in a more poker-faced manner. Upon entering a room full of people, women will fre-

Women tend to have higher levels of nonverbal communication than do men, and there are physiological reasons for that. Women have about 11 percent more neurons in the areas of the brain responsible for language and hearing. In women, the hippocampus—the center for memory and emotion—is larger than it is in men.

---

6   Ibid

7   Ibid

quently begin greeting people while looking them directly in the eye, while men will lower their eyes or simply scan the room.

As we acknowledge that women tend to use more nonverbal modes of communication, it's also important to understand that while these signals are often interpreted correctly by other women, they're often misread by men. A women's direct eye contact, smiles, and effusive gestures can be processed by men as a low-power form of communication.

Most women already have the facility to adapt to circumstances as needed. Powerful Women Speak encourages them to adapt their tone to today's workplace. The tone of any message is just as important as the message being delivered. Peter Drucker, the father of modern business, wisely said: "The most important thing in communication is hearing what isn't said."

Let's look at the trap many women find themselves in. If they're too nice, they're perceived as weak. If they're too strong, they're perceived as controlling. A very direct woman is seen as edgy. The challenge is to be aware of perceptions and say, "I'm not going to just communicate the way I'm naturally wired to. I'm going to assess who it is I'm communicating with and what message I want to get across—and then I'm going to adapt my delivery to those circum- stances so it can have the maximum impact."

Good communication is more than words. How many times has the message been correct but the tone in which it was delivered wrong? For instance, women may communicate in a motherly tone in the workplace, using endearments such as *dear* and *hon*. But people are at work—that type of motherly communication should be left at home.

So, what can women do to communicate from a place of power? They can curtail their use of the word *just*. Ellen Petry Leanse, who has worked with Google and Apple, suggested that just is viewed as a permission word, a word whose meaning boils down to "sorry to bother you."[8] Think about it: "I just want to check on you" versus "I want to check on you." Or "I was just wondering whether you had decided" versus the more direct "Have you decided?"

Women are biologically and socially wired to preserve relationships, and that entails minimizing conflict when communicating.[9] The word just is perfectly suited to that purpose, and women tend to use it much more than men.

> What can women do to communicate from a place of power? They can curtail their use of the word just.

Unfortunately, interjecting that simple word into email and verbal conversations can communicate lower power and set women up to be taken less seriously than their male counterparts.

Another recommended action is for women to focus more on the use of the word *I* and less on the word *we*. *I* is a positive achievement word. "I did this" versus "We did this." This touches on the related idea of women speaking up for themselves, understanding that their hard work deserves recognition. Perhaps most importantly, women need to understand that if they want something, they shouldn't assume their boss or business associates know what it is; they should directly verbalize the action that they wish to be taken.

It's also helpful for women to take things less personally. Whereas men have an innate ability to analyze feedback factually and then move on, women may be haunted by—and unable to let go

---

8   Ellen Petry Leanse, "Google and Apple alum says using this word can damage your credibility," Business Insider, June 25, 2015, https://www.businessinsider. com/former-google-exec-says-this-word-can-damage-your-credibility-2015-6.

9   Maureen Sander-Staudt, "Care Ethics," Internet Encyclopedia of Philosophy, https://www.iep.utm.edu/care-eth.

of—the same type of feedback. When you take constructive criticism personally, it's difficult to process it correctly. Consider the feedback provided and the changes that need to be made, then develop a plan to improve and move forward.

Women can communicate more effectively in the workplace by processing options internally. In a group setting, women may make decisions about the best way for their project to progress by weighing various options aloud. In a meeting room, women may say, "Well, we could do it this way because . . ." and, "But then again, we might consider what so-and-so said."

This is another type of communication that men can process as low power. Men may go through that same dialogue, but typically they do it in their heads. What a man says aloud is, "I've looked at the choices, and I've decided to go with option A." While talking out options is, in reality, simply another style of processing, it can easily be perceived as waffling, as coming from a place of weakness and indecision. Processing options is an important part of making good decisions—just don't process in front of an audience.

Listening neutrally is another communication solution for women to consider. When I'm presenting new ideas to a group, invariably I'll see women nodding their heads—while the bulk of the men in the audience show no physical reaction to what I'm saying. When heads nod, it may just be that the women are processing—indicating that they understand the concept. But a man may perceive a nod as a sign of agreement.

I encourage women to optimize networking situations by staying focused on why they're there. The purpose of networking is to create a positive image and make connections. Many women network from a position of "trouble talk." They use common challenges as a way to build a bridge to others. You'll hear phrases such as "I have these concerns at work" and "I'm finding it a challenge to maintain good care for my children at home." Men in similar networking situations start to peel away—this isn't what they're there for.

What men tend to do in networking circumstances, and what women should do, is think and speak about successes they've had, projects they've led. Powerful people tend to interact with those who have positive things to share. They use—and expect to hear—that I word.

Think about attending a company meeting. What dynamics occur when attendees are asked to share their opinions? Who speaks first? In a meeting or other group setting with business associates, it is important to speak up—and to speak up early. The best message to deliver is one that reflects on the points heard earlier in the meeting, but also firmly presents a unique opinion. "I've considered everything you've said, and I have an idea that could take the company in a different direction. Let me share it with you."

Women may hesitate and wait until several people have spoken up, and then they will offer their input. Often what occurs is that someone will already have said what they were going to say, so when they're called on, their comment is, "I agree with Bill." But they could have spoken up earlier and been the one to give an original contribution to the conversation. I challenge women to be thoughtful about how and when they speak up—and to do so at the front end of the question-and-answer session rather than at the back end.

In the workplace, it's necessary to handle conflict constructively. If you're giving negative feedback to an employee, or if you're discussing a matter you expect the other party to react negatively to, it's important not to be wishy-washy. Be direct, concrete, and honest. State the expected outcome up front so there's no room for misinterpretation. Sometimes, we attempt to soften the message. The effect of this can be the other person not fully understanding what we're trying to say.

A tool to further enhance speaking power is for women, at the end of critical discussion meetings, to summarize: "This is what we spoke about. This is the outcome that should come from that. This needs to stop by this date or I need to have this project done by this date in this way. Are you in agreement?"

Sometimes, women are viewed as passive-aggressive. They go along with things they're not comfortable with because they don't want to be confrontational, when it would be far better to say, "I understand your opinion, but I'm looking at it in another way and I'd like to go down that path," or, "I'd like the meeting to start at two, not twelve, for this reason." Rather than being passive-aggressive, it is more effective to state clearly what you want.

Women can be effective communicators in the workplace. Women can understand communication differences and enhance the way they relate with men and other women. People who communicate from a place of strength are empowered and show authority, which ultimately comes from being prepared for whatever topic you're speaking about or meeting you're holding. Using these tools, a woman can find her own natural style of communicating—one that is firm and direct.

Recognizing the verbal and nonverbal signals you send takes practice, as does learning to speak with power. Fortunately, there are many current and historical examples—from Oprah Winfrey to Sheryl Sandberg, Angela Merkel to Margaret Thatcher—of women communicating their messages clearly, without apology or self-doubt. By adopting the suggestions encompassed in Powerful Women Speak, female business entrepreneurs, managers, and women in the workplace can learn to communicate with that same self-assured clarity and make themselves heard!

ACCESSING YOUR COMPANY'S EFFICIENCIES

PERRY ADLER, CFO, AMARYLLIS DESIGN

Upon joining the floral and event design firm Amaryllis as chief financial officer, it was my challenge to find efficiencies that could be made accessible to the company. First, I focused on gaining a thorough understanding of the company culture and how operations were handled, getting a handle on how those two important areas converged. Doing this was step one in spearheading the company's growth.

To comprehend how we grew and what solutions worked for us, it's important to know where the company came from. Amaryllis was started nearly three decades ago in the basement of the Omni Shoreham Hotel in Washington, DC. They did a stellar job with centerpieces, bouquets, floral arrangements—you name it. If it concerned flowers, they handled it. Before long, what had begun as a four-person operation had grown exponentially.

Expansion continued until Amaryllis occupied four different facilities, all in the DC area. But this situation soon proved chaotic: four sites, but inventory in one and designers spread across the others. In 2013, the company moved everything—all operations and inventory—to a 50,000-square-foot warehouse in Landover, Maryland. This is where the company operates today.

Amaryllis recruited me on the basis of my background—accounting, with a side of HR, policy, and procedural implementation. I brought with me an upper-management decision-making aptitude. After a couple weeks of back-and-forth negotiations, I came on board, as I was intrigued by what they could offer me: being a big fish in a small pond, with the corresponding level of responsibility. The challenge was appealing.

Upon joining the team, I quickly found a couple of issues. First, there was a lack of policies and procedures. Second, there was a distinct division between the art mentality and business mentality. There was a blue-collar employee base in the warehouse—starkly separated from the creative-minded designers who had gone to art school.

Getting down to specifics, I discovered there were several efficiency metrics that weren't really being monitored or accounted for. From the get-go, we needed to start looking at head count, payroll, and ratios related to the type of money coming in the door. Within three months of being hired, I had completed my initial analysis. I met with the owner and suggested that we were somewhat top-heavy—and probably needed to get rid of some people if we were going to operate efficiently. We ended up doing a layoff.

Sometimes, people ride the coattails of a growing business even though their jobs are rarely relevant.

I wasn't happy about this—no one enjoys that process—but it was necessary for streamlining operations. Sometimes, people ride the coattails of a growing business even though their jobs are rarely relevant, and that was the case here. However, I did try to transition people as easily as possible. When people get terminated, they usually don't receive any type of package, but we made it a priority to offer a severance package. This was in December 2014.

Naturally, the owner and upper management understood the necessity of what I was doing. They supported me. Soon, they were able to reap the fruits of my efforts, as the layoffs freed up funds from payroll that were then reinvested elsewhere in the company.

One of the primary ways in which we reinvested—and also one of the strongest measurable areas of growth attributable to my coming on board—was purchasing more inventory. We made room in the warehouse for it so that we could service an expanding and diverging customer base.

Another area of need I noticed involved operations—they weren't streamlined. Everybody was in a silo, with no system integration and poor interdepartmental communication. Salespeople operated individually and stored their proposals on their own hard drives, meaning there was no systematic, centralized storage of proposals and other sales material. An in-house network existed, but it was underutilized.

The upshot of this was an occluded view of what the sales force was doing day to day. There was no paradigm for unified pricing—each salesperson proposed their own terms. While there's nothing wrong with salespeople trying to make good margins, when management can't see what they're doing, it is difficult to assess what margins are realistic for a given product or service.

I saw unifying all this data as a way to establish a shared playing field for all individuals and all teams. The first system introduced was a simple customer relation management (CRM) tool, which blew up into a huge enterprise-resource solution. This system eventually allowed us to produce proposals at a much faster rate—without losing finesse.

The ability to streamline operations so dramatically hinges on the same principle behind all efforts to access efficiencies: You must understand the needs of the particular business you're in. Our proposals, for instance, are different from those you might see in a lot of other businesses because we do not incorporate photos. Our salespeople rely on eloquent prose to paint vivid images in clients' minds.

These proposals—which take real craftsmanship and require sales staff to get "in the zone"—could take four, six, or even eight hours to create, depending on the size of the event. And our events could range in price from $10,000 to $750,000. As necessary as these proposals were to our business, they were also time killers. We needed to systemize the process so a salesperson could basically just push out a proposal without losing their creative edge.

The system we created, nicknamed the "Sales Proposal Wizard," does this by remembering the mechanics of the salesperson's pitch. It then incorporates custom descriptive paragraphs dreamed up by the salesperson, who then formulates it into a polished, customer-ready proposal. This customized CRM tool cuts the author's time expenditure by up to 75 percent.

The system also allows our sales teams to tap into unified pricing and available-to-promise (ATP) for any of our hundred thousand different inventory pieces—ranging from small votive candles all the way up to couches, bars, and even large walls, chandeliers, and overhangs. From that point, the system takes over accounting functions and creates an invoice that can be emailed directly to the client from the Salesforce platform. No longer does the accounting department have to manually create an invoice from a folder containing notes and various revisions given to them by the sales teams. This has aided us greatly, not only saving time but also improving accuracy.

Another challenge we faced was our limited ability for sales and production teams to follow the accounting department and note when client deposits were received—which triggered the ordering of materials and scheduling of labor. Our new CRM system eliminated the old-fashioned need to call or email back and forth between departments about whether a payment had been received.

These upgrades and improvements addressed operations: how we sold, how we kept tabs on accounting, and how departments within the company communicated with one another. And these are areas owners of any small- to medium-sized business should comb through carefully—there are frequently inefficiencies that can be located and remedied.

Another key area that required improved efficiency was our production house. As the business grew, we often had to bring in inventory outside the floral component in order to make custom goods for clients. When we designed events, it wasn't just a matter of bringing the latest in-fashion Hermes couch to a party.

On one occasion, we had someone who wanted to walk atop their pool at their wedding—to literally walk on water. This meant constructing Lucite podiums that would sit in the pool and could withstand shaking and vigorous movement. Another job saw us build something reminiscent of a large, historic 1930s speakeasy that was housed outdoors in a 100 x 50-foot tent—situated on the shifting sand of a beach on Nantucket. This complex structure needed to be built to spec, then dismantled, shipped in various trucks/boats to the site, and put back together quickly—while retaining structural integrity.

Bigger projects such as these were handled in-house by our carpenters and welders, who held down the fort in the carpentry department. Our production house also included artists such as painters and industrial sewers in the textiles department.

When we were tasked with building something intricate or large, our timeline could easily become quite long. Take the simple example of a couch. It starts in carpentry, then goes to the paint crew, and then to textiles for upholstery. Naturally, some of these steps involve lag time; for instance, paint has to cure before anyone can lay their hands on the couch to upholster it.

The tight schedules we were frequently under in event design weren't amenable to this long production process. It's an area where the company had lost a great deal of money in the past—which meant it was an area I looked at carefully to find inefficiencies and solutions for them.

In my assessment, I found problems with communication between departments. Details were missed because there wasn't a true standard of communication—key instructions might be jotted on a notepad, but it wasn't certain if the right person would consult it, and sometimes they were lost. Other times, side conversations took place about the details of the build—but then the details were forgotten. On top of all this, people weren't in the habit of verifying that the departments that were receiving the instructions were correctly inter-preting those messages.

Many inefficiencies stemmed from this core communication problem. The company incurred added expense from having to order materials overnight because they hadn't been ordered in a timely manner, or place a second order because the first contained errors. Labor costs were also adversely affected, as we sometimes had teams working night after night after night to complete a project.

We were able to access efficiencies by building systems to monitor all custom builds, then implementing a visible production workflow. With these measures, we got everybody on the same page by having them work with the same notebook. We outfitted each department with giant monitors displaying what was next in the pipeline, along with any upcoming deadlines.

The final stage of customizing this new system was to create a portal for asset management, tagging the rentable inventory pieces with radio-frequency identification (RFID) transmitters. This allows management know whether an asset is available to rent, what its price is, how many times the item has been rented, the breakability of the item, how many units are on hand, and so on. And previously unavailable metrics can now be obtained—which has led to better knowledge of our inventory and given us the insight to make better purchasing decisions.

This communication system that I designed and built has far-reaching implications—it really taps into the core of how many companies operate. Because it focuses on what drives the business, what the key elements are, what's causing problems, and how to ultimately find efficiencies, I see it as applicable to many different industries. In fact, people have said to me, "You know, you should quit this job and go on tour, just implementing this across the world."

THESE ARE THE KEY ELEMENTS FOR MAKING THIS PROJECT A SUCCESSFUL ENDEAVOR:

1. Understand the process—what works and (just as important) what doesn't work. What are the inefficiencies based on time, labor, material, quality, or whatever metrics are key to your company? Where do you and your team, as experts, need

to improve?

2. Create cultural changes in steps that your company's workforce is able to accommodate.

3. Strategize the change in order to create buy-in from key individuals or departments so they truly understand the need to better the process. These process managers will become advocates for the cause, having the same vision as you in the finished product and how it will improve the company.

While the basics of the system I've described could benefit many industries, all CFOs must ascertain the facts on the ground of the businesses they work for. They have to look at what causes the owners or management the most grief and where the areas of inefficiency are. Where is the company spending the most time? Where is it spending the most money? Where does it need the best ROI? These questions are all important to ask because a more standardized inventory and manufacturing process will equal an ROI being received much, much faster.

I've noticed that many new companies started by millennials begin with these well-thought-out, streamlined systems of operation already in place. I would recommend this practice to all new business owners. It's more expensive to put these tools in place after the fact, when you're accustomed doing things in ways that grew organically and are often less efficient. It can also be difficult to accept the idea that a systems overhaul is needed—particularly if the business is already successful *enough*.

With Amaryllis, I became a sort of change manager, coming into a company that was already successful. I hadn't made it a success, and I had to convince them that a change of this magnitude was warranted. I faced the expected resistance; it was a successful company, so why mess with it? Why go changing things? Getting the buy-in was difficult; I had to really sell the idea.

One thing that helped me was my strong belief in the system I was proposing, as I knew that every little step could be quantitatively shown to add to the bottom line. Yes, new systems can be expensive, so keep your eye on the scope of the project and what you set out to achieve in the first place. Once you've achieved that, measure your ROI before the next big systematic endeavor.

In business, you always have to judge the systems you adopt—the solutions you put in place—against the numbers. For companies in our industry, good margins are typically 6 to 8 percent. We're now looking at taking margins from 6 to about 18 percent. I attribute this, by and large, to finding efficiencies in a cost-heavy business.

A dynamic, evolving business will always have new challenges. It's true that the project of designing and building up a streamlined operations system will present challenges of its own. There's always an adjustment period, a learning curve. That's why whatever the inefficiencies are—and however specifically they're being corrected—it's important to keep in mind why you're doing all this.

The motivation has to be adding long-term growth and value. If you're fixing your company's inefficiencies, you're enhancing a product to make it more manageable—more streamlined, more

> *In business, you always have to judge the systems you adopt—the solutions you put in place— against the numbers.*

controlled. If you ultimately want to sell the business, your streamlining efforts will result in a turnkey product that can add millions to your asking price down the road. In the shorter term, you'll speed up your ROI, cut down the timeline for completing a given task, and improve communications across your business.

When designed properly, your improved system of operations will help you monitor all the right metrics—and thereby make smart decisions about your company's future, all the while adding intrinsic value to your company and improving its bottom line. Cheers to those who are up to the challenge!

FUEL YOUR BUSINESS WITH PASSION AND PRINCIPLES: CONFESSIONS OF A CEO OF A SERVANT-LEADERSHIP TECHNOLOGY COMPANY

ELIZABETH HESS, CEO,
BULLSEYE COMPUTING

Having grown up in China during the Cultural Revolution, where food was rationed and people barely made enough money to live on, I vividly recall numerous occasions when my grandmother generously helped family and friends, like Mrs. Xu, a single mother of two, who had lost her husband to illness. I remember people in tears, thanking my grandmother, while she reassured them in a soft and gentle voice that everything was going to be okay. On those nights of such giving, my grandparents would have a quiet discussion on how we would get by over the rest of that month on a much-reduced budget.

Whether inherited or learned, I too have found great pleasure in making others happy—even if it means going out of my way, sometimes *way* out of my way.

As a teenager, I fell madly in love with computers, particularly software programming. I spent all of my free time programming—well, sometimes borrowed time from geography or communist-theory classes. The risk was great, but worth it. I loved how computers did exactly what I programmed them to do; I loved how they silently served and never complained. After high school, I was fortunate enough to come to the United States to study computer science. I didn't waste any time, earning two degrees, a bachelor's and a master's back to back in the computing field.

But never in my wildest dreams did I imagine that one day I would be the head of a technology company, let alone one that so closely aligned to my greatest passion. It was as if I had married the field I loved. I raced to join the workforce the last semester in graduate school, anxious to put my skills to use. I was a happy camper during the initial honeymoon period, until I was promoted to Manager of Systems Engineering. It was here I was instructed by the CEO about how to lie to customers and treat engineers as commodities, because "they all could be easily replaced." With each software release, the conflict between my core values and those of the CEO's grew. I felt so much stress that I thought for sure I would be having a heart attack at work soon. Following the leader got me to a place where I did not belong. So I left.

Soon after that, on a sunny January afternoon twenty years ago, in the state of Maryland, I cofounded a boutique IT company called BullsEye Computing Solutions; its name resonates with our conviction to do things right the first time. We founded BullsEye to provide quality products to its customers—and to take good care of its employees. That afternoon, I became an "instant CEO."

Little did I know that I was in way over my head. As a product of the Chinese Cultural Revolution—an era not dissimilar to George Orwell's 1984—I was raised to keep my mouth shut and express no ideas that might be considered unique or radical. I was a good student, a follower—deathly afraid of being the first girl in my class to wear a summer dress when the weather turned hot. Being a CEO, a leader whom everyone else was expecting to follow—well, that just was not my cup of tea.

I spent many years searching for the Holy Grail for BullsEye. I'd hope, then hope some more, that maybe the salesperson walking through the door would be it, or the next technological trend, or the next brilliant engineer that I hired. Something that would lead the company to greatness. Many of these people and trends came and went, but the company—and me? We were stuck in molasses. At one point, even that startup monster of negative cash flow came and tried to swallow us up.

After what seemed like a plethora of mistakes and failed attempts—mixed in with the occasional successful project that came along with unpredictable timing and some profits—I finally realized that, although I was the CEO on paper, deep down I was still a follower. That's why I was not able to set BullsEye sailing in the right direction. Once that light bulb came on, it seemed so ridiculously obvious to me that if BullsEye was to be successful, I as CEO must become a true leader. I had to lead it in a way that matches who I am, not who anyone else is—or wants me to be.

> *If BullsEye was to be successful, I as CEO must become a true leader. I had to lead it in a way that matches who I am, not who anyone else is—or wants me to be.*

Thus began my journey of self-discovery and organizational transformation. Along the way, I met many local business leaders and coaches who were inspirational to me over the years. I also joined the Baltimore, Maryland, chapter of TAB, whose peer advisory boards, DISC profiling, and subsequent coaching sessions proved to be of great value to me.

Know Thyself

I might have known all along what my natural styles were, but I never really laid them out on the table and took a hard look at them—perhaps out of fear that they might not mesh with being the CEO of a tech company. Now that I have determined that, as a CEO, my natural style and fundamental principles will be the driving force shaping our corporate mission, vision, culture, and ultimately, its success—I am able to self-reflect (with the help of DISC profiling and TAB coaching sessions).

These were my key findings and my admissions about myself:

- I will go out of my way to help other people and see them well, happy, and successful.

- I love to solve challenging problems and make a difference.

- I am a perfectionist when it comes to quality of work and customer dedication.

- I lead by consensus, enjoy team harmony, an am forgiving and easy-going.

- I am an eternal optimist who sees the glass as always half full, never half empty.

- I love being a mentor and sharing knowledge and experience

A couple of new traits have emerged after living for three

decades in America and being married to a redheaded boy from Richmond, Virginia:

- From having no opinion about anything, I now have an opinion about everything!

- I have a sense of heightened creativity: not the timid, forced kind from China, but the innovative, dare-to-be-different kind.

- I have the guts to own up to things when they go wrong—without losing composure or dignity for anyone or myself.

Servant-Leadership Fueled by Passion and Principles

Once the self-assessment was done, it did not take long to figure out that BullsEye was destined to become a full-fledged servant-leadership company—because that is where its CEO's passion and core principles lie.

Whether we provided software applications or consulting services to our customers became less relevant. Our mission was to be laser focused on bringing measurable success to our customers. Sure, you might say, every company pitches that it wants to see its customers succeed. So how is BullsEye different? Well, it took some soul searching, and a lot of planning, for me to change our mission from "We leverage technology to help our customers succeed" to "We *guarantee* customer success through technology and human resources empowerment." Why use a strong word like *guarantee*? To differentiate us, of course, in the world of IT—where slippery words like It depends are much preferred to a scary one like *guarantee*. But most importantly, I want our team to pledge guaranteed success to our customers, who have put their trust and sometimes their careers on the line to recommend BullsEye over the big firms.

For many years, like every other company, we referred to our customers as our Partners. We pitched win–win strategies. But the conviction of being a servant-leadership organization made me question whether there was a better way to describe our relationship with our customers. Partnership implies that both parties have something to gain, thus they get together to do something. At first it makes you think, "What's in it for me?"

So, instead, I decided BullsEye and its customers would be "Best Friends." It makes both sides feel warm and fuzzy, much like how I felt when I saw my best friend every morning at school. No matter what happened, I knew she'd always understood and been there for me. I knew if I asked for her opinion, she would give me an honest answer—because she had my best interests at heart. While "Best Friends" may sound strange or even scary to some, those two words clearly express to our customers that they should expect every encounter, every experience with BullsEye to be a positive one.

> *While "Best Friends" may sound strange or even scary to some, those two words clearly express to our customers that they should expect every encounter, every experience with BullsEye to be a positive one.*

The Need to Serve More

Being a servant-leader set a new course for BullsEye and me. I no longer wake up every day wondering where the next project will come from. Instead, I get up energized and wondering who we can help, and with whom I would be privileged to work with or talk to. Interestingly enough, after this, business started to steadily grow.

I must confess that there does exist a flip side to this servant-leadership thing. That is, one person can only serve, at the most, a few *best friends*. With the growth we were experiencing, it became clear that I needed help. Through trial and error and some growing pains, I learned the following:

- I needed to have a team of competent servant–leaders who were experienced and passionate about what they were doing

- as a CEO, not only did I serve my customers, I also had to serve all of those who worked with me.

Today, I make sure that everyone on the BullsEye team is a servant-leader—ready to support their colleagues and to serve our customers. I never considered that the employees or contractors of BullsEye worked *for* me. Instead, they work *with* me to serve our customers. So, in turn, I serve them, support them, and remove obstacles for them. I make sure their needs are taken care of in a way that goes far beyond a paycheck.

In my extended Chinese family, there often are disagreements and conflicts. But harmony reigns over my BullsEye family, not because we all have the same personality or natural working style. To the contrary, some of us have similar traits that enhance each other, while others have dissimilar traits that complement each other. As an example, in my constant quest to do things perfectly, I often neglect the fact that project deadlines are approaching. A few veteran project managers whom I serve with, who are always very much focused on the details—such as the due dates of projects—serve their group members and the customers by complementing my weakness/ tardiness with their strength in schedule management.

There have been many occasions when customers were very

surprised to learn that another BullsEye team member was collaborating with me, even though the person had been with us for only a short time. They were convinced by the way we worked and interacted with one another that we had been working together for at least a decade or two.

Go the Extra Mile

Most companies talk about going the extra mile for their customers, but how many really do? Moreover, how many are willing to do it time after time, year after year? Not that many. Why not?

Most of the big companies are too big to go through it, while the smaller firms are often too afraid to go down this questionable side street marked "Extra Mile." But being a servant-leadership company, BullsEye has been able to successfully go that Extra Mile with family and friends, as a unified group with common goals and a collaborative spirit. We all know how sunny it is at the other end of that Extra Mile; that's why our customers and team members stay with us, turning many short-term engagements into long-term friendship.

Mixing Business with Pleasure

Delivering enterprise solutions and services is challenging. Being the CEO of an IT company, the one with whom the buck stops, means I carry a tremendous weight on my shoulders. But among the challenges and obstacles, I am also having a blast. I am a firm believer in mixing business with pleasure (within regulatory compliance boundaries). What could be better than getting up every morning to collaborate and hangout with your "family and friends," doing what you have loved for thirty-plus years, and making a difference? I have achieved what I have because I followed my passion, my principles, and my natural management style as a servant–leader. This is my story. It may help you, but certainly is not for everyone.

Find your passion, dreams, and your styles. Create your own BullsEye!

RECRUITING SMARTER

BRAD LEAHY, VICE PRESIDENT AND
OWNER, BLADES OF GREEN

People always say, "I can't find good help. No one wants
to work anymore. Millennials are lazy." And if it's not the millennials,
it's another group. The fill-in-the-blank generation is lazy, according
to many people, and that's why they can't recruit the right employees.
The other major excuse I hear is the unemployment rate is so low that
people can't find good employees. I have news for you. Of the people
we hired last year, 89 percent were already employed.

But I've come to the conclusion that the lazy generation is ours.
We—the people doing the hiring, the business owners—are the ones
slacking. It's not the fault of the millennials or those of "generation
whatever." It is we who haven't
adapted; we need to adapt to the
way they're ready to be recruited,
hired, and trained.

> We need to adapt to
> the way they're ready
> to be recruited,
> hired, and trained.

This is a problem we've faced
head on in my business, Blades of
Green. We had difficulty recruiting frontline, entry-level positions—

particularly since we're in the service industry of lawn care and pest control. It's not sexy; there's no glamour. You don't tend to hear twelve-year-olds saying, "When I grow up, I want to be a lawn care or pest control technician."

Through a team effort, though, we discovered a three-point process for successfully recruiting and hiring. The first key is that we treat our recruiting and hiring process just like we do sales and marketing. There's a thought process that goes into acquiring a new customer. What's the acquisition cost? What's our close rate on that customer? How long does that customer stay?

In our recruiting and hiring process, we ask similar questions. How many applicants does it take to hire one person? What was the lead source that drove that applicant to apply? How long did a hire, based on which ad they responded to, stay with the company? What, specifically, did the ad say?

We generate a lot of our new customers from pay-per-click advertising, in which we use about five words—just a snippet—to convince the customer to click. Recruiting should be treated the same way. Both advertising and recruiting material should be memorable enough to generate interest.

For our business, we've found that creative ads win out. Sure, we've tried typical, straightforward "technician needed" ads—and we still have those ads in circulation. However, we've found greater success with ads that focus on career aspirations or use intriguing wording. Ads that say, for example, "If you lack a sense of humor, please do not click on this opportunity," or, "Are you handy? Do you enjoy dancing in the rain? Does building a snowman excite you? Were you the kid killing bugs with the magnifying glass?"

Your next opportunity comes when a potential applicant clicks on the title of the ad. What they read next needs to live up to the promise of the teaser text. Take this example:

If you answered yes to any of these questions, you might be a fit for this award-winning company. We like working outside with our hands and having fun. With 29 years of experience in our region, we dare you to find a company more committed to its people, its service, and its clients.

Then we would detail our accomplishments, finishing with a call to action. "What are you waiting for?"

If you're stuck trying to come up with creative, relevant ads—if the person in charge of hiring is perhaps not the company's most creative writer—then I recommend having a contest. Invite everyone to submit a job ad, with the winner getting a prize. Our business analyst, a numbers cruncher, wrote our most successful ad last year.

When I give presentations on this subject, I like to ask business owners how much revenue an average technician generates over their term of employment. Answers can range from $1 million to $3 million. At a 10 percent profit, you're looking at a figure somewhere between $100,000 and $300,000. The question I try to get business owners to ask themselves is this: "How much are you willing to spend on the person who can generate that amount for you?" And while these sharp business minds always do this sort of equation for potential customers, they're not used to applying the same thought process to recruits.

Another way in which you need to treat potential recruits like potential customers involves response time. In our office, if you call in to buy something, the response time is immediate. However, when I encounter business owners who say they have a hard time finding good workers and I ask, "What is your response time when someone does apply?" They'll typically say, "Oh, maybe a week. Maybe a day." I always tell them the same thing, "Your response should be immediate."

Key number two is you need the data to do all of this for you: Figure out what will work for your industry, your location, your applicant pool. In other words, you need an applicant tracking system.

Your system can be as simple as an Excel spreadsheet—or it can be much more sophisticated. The important thing is that you have something to help you keep up with a list of names, indicate what job-listing source the applicants responded to (Craigslist, Indeed, CareerBuilder, LinkedIn, etc.), and so forth. You will use all this data to look back at your hires and analyze what worked and what didn't. How much did each recruit cost? Was a given source of leads effective, or not?

We use professional-service software that actually tells us which ad a recruit clicked and what that ad said. It tracks that person for their entire life with the company. If a team member leaves us after ten years, we can look back at the ad that generated their interest. And if someone stays for only three, six, or nine months, we would want to acknowledge that this wasn't a successful campaign—again, the same approach you would take to advertising.

The third key is a good company culture. I like to get people thinking about how an applicant will get to know a company they might want to work for. Say you've got a great recruiting system and a strong ad that drives interest. They click it, they read it, they're intrigued. What happens next?

This potential recruit goes to your website or your social media profile to see what everyone thinks of you. If you have bad reviews online, or if your website is outdated, or if there's not overwhelming visual proof of a good company culture, then you're likely to lose that recruit's interest.

This is why your website is of the utmost importance. This is your space to display pictures of charity work, company outings, team-building exercises, training, and other types of employee activities outside the workplace. And note that I said *overwhelming* visual proof. One picture of a holiday party from ten years ago won't cut it.

You need post after post, picture after picture, video after video. When a potential recruit goes to your website or social media platform, they need to see evidence of a company culture that clearly has not been "produced." You need to show them these are your real employees, attending and enjoying real company events.

What we've learned about the people who are interested in our entry-level, skilled-labor jobs is they want to work outside and they want to work with their hands. Most importantly, they want to work for a company that treats them well and offers a good culture. The thing that makes us a better option than other, similar service companies is our culture—of which applicants find ample visual proof.

We've found, upon surveying new hires, that they also take customer reviews into account. Simply put, they want to work for a company whose values and quality of work match theirs. They want to be able to stand behind whatever product or service they represent. They need to see that the company does the same.

Obviously, even a company that provides a valuable service, does high-quality work, and cares about the customer experience isn't immune to bad reviews. This is where the importance of review management comes into play. Essentially, you want to make sure that you respond appropriately to a customer complaint; if you don't, the candidate will get the wrong impression. Your response gives your side and helps write the company's story—not the disgruntled customer's or employee's.

The concept of visual proof should extend to your physical location as well. When a new applicant walks in our door, they immediately see awards and news articles written about us. We've been among the Inc. 5000 fastest-growing companies in our area for the last two years. They see those commendations, along with employee-of-the-month and employee-of-the-year awards.

If you go to the "careers" section of most websites, you'll probably see a job feed and perhaps a paragraph or so of company history. Our careers section goes on for six or seven pages. One page, of course, lists jobs; the remaining pages focus on the people at our company and what they like to do. This shows applicants what kind of people they'll be working with, what our culture is all about, what our vision is, and what our values are.

In this space, it's important to include video proof as well. If video isn't king already, it soon will be. If I can video a current team member's testimonial instead of putting a picture of them next to a written quote, it feels much more authentic. Everybody knows you can get a picture of a decent-looking, average person from the Internet and write whatever you want next to it—that's why video is more persuasive. So we capture videos of employees saying why they like working for us.

Our careers page also goes into fun stuff, like how many people on the team are left-handed versus right-handed, what kind of pets everyone has, etc. Research has shown that 70 percent of millennials own pets, so we show them they'd be coming to work in a pet-friendly culture.

The system I've outlined here for recruiting and hiring doesn't just sound nice on paper—the numbers back it up. Before we started it approximately five years ago, our yearly retention rate for frontline employees was somewhere around 35 percent—in an industry where the average is somewhere in the 65 percent range. Under our new system, we're currently retaining 80 percent. Additionally, this year we've reduced our cost per hire by 40 percent from last year.

If business owners want results similar to the ones we've seen, I advise them to stop whining about millennials and get to work. Follow the tried and tested points I've outlined here, and stick to a detailed hiring process—a written, step-by-step, check-listed process that the company adheres to consistently.

We have a centralized system with our HR team getting everybody through the beginning stages—just to get qualified. To be considered, you have to make it through 80 percent of the process. Then the direct report manager gets involved, along with the HR team or person responsible for hiring, who is always present to ensure consistency.

> *If business owners want results similar to the ones we've seen, I advise them to stop whining about millennials and get to work.*

Our process would be very difficult for someone to get through by lying. In person and on the phone, applicants go over résumé, application, testing, interviews, etc. We ask the same questions over and over and over, and if we get inconsistent answers, we know we have a problem.

I've met business leaders who officially have these processes in place—but … no one in the company follows them. I see it all the time. Branch managers in different areas hire in entirely different ways. Everyone wonders why there's a problem when it comes to bringing new people on board.

From the first step of the recruiting process to the last step of hiring, it's important to remember that there's nothing wrong with millennials—or any other generation. There are plenty of hard workers with well-honed skill sets out there, and you'll find them if you do your job as a business owner and recruit well.

PERSONAL ENGAGEMENT
WITH YOUR TEAM

LEO FOX, CEO AND FOUNDER,
VECTOR CONSULTING

I like to say that we at Tenacity Solutions were in cybersecurity before it was sexy. And it certainly became sexy!

For quite some time now, many of the names in cybersecurity have belonged to the big guys—meaning the field is sometimes seen as unfriendly terrain for small to medium-sized businesses. You could really observe this after 9/11, when many big companies started gobbling up the little guys, and the little guys started taking deals. The bigger fish had, in fact, gone on a wild spending spree by the time I cofounded Tenacity Solutions with my wife, Mary, and longtime friend and business partner, Matt Wilmoth, in 2003.

We founded the company as a small information technology firm catering to, among other clientele, the US intelligence community. Within six years we had made Inc. magazine's 2009 list of the fastest-growing private firms, and we continued making that list every year until we sold the company in 2014.

My own background included working for Creative Technology Incorporated as director of IT programs for the intelligence community. Prior to that, I directed the Network Integration Division of CTX, which I cofounded. I began my career serving as a telecommunications security officer in the CIA, working with both their communications and security divisions after graduating from the Citadel.

While my prior training and experience were obviously useful at Tenacity, another factor helped us stand out and survive in a sector so rife with competition: luck. Matt and I were lucky to be trusted early on with a couple of large contracts. While luck is invariably going to play a role in any business success, you have to be ready to capitalize on it when it comes your way.

I should also add the caveat that what most of us consider luck—fortuitously timed opportunity—came from our previous extremely hard work. It was ultimately our earlier work that encouraged new clients with large contracts to trust us. When we delivered on those first contracts, we inspired more faith in Tenacity, which allowed us to build from there.

> While luck is invariably going to play a role in any business success, you have to be ready to capitalize on it when it comes your way.

Another substantial differentiator—perhaps the most important one—was in how we treated our employees. I cannot overstate the importance of making your employees—as well as their significant others—feel like an integrated part of the team, which in turn helps them feel ownership over the product or service they're representing.

When I say we prioritized our employees and their relationship with the company, I don't mean that in an abstract sense—it wasn't a nice thought that existed only in buzzword language used to promote the company. It was a matter of policy. We could break it down into numbers. We gave equity to everyone at a time when it was rare for businesses of our size and focus to do so. All of our employees received employer-funded comprehensive benefits packages along with semiannual bonuses. Not only that, but we paid employees for every hour they worked, which incentivized them to work on a project as long and hard as necessary.

Employees are always going to perform their best for a company where they feel they have a stake—and a voice—and where the higher-ups seem to genuinely care. That's why I strongly recommend setting aside corporate funds for company retreats—ultimately doing so is an investment. Every year we would shut down the company and invite all employees and their significant others to off-site retreats where we would celebrate corporate achievements and plan for the future. We also hosted Christmas parties that were welcoming and fun for employees' families.

Besides ensuring that the people who work for you are well provided for in terms of pay and benefits—and that they're acknowledged for their contributions—you need to mentor them. Fortunately, both Matt and I had a passion for getting the company's next generation ready to go. We both considered it vital to show our team members we were paying attention to them individually and that they had access to us when they needed it.

As part of our mentoring efforts, we encouraged employees to learn, both on and off the job. From early on in Tenacity's history

Employees are always going to perform their best for a company where they feel they have a stake—and a voice—and where the higher-ups seem to genuinely care.

we ran Next Generation Leadership classes. These classes, run after hours, would train our employees on subjects such as project management, business development, and proposal writing—to mention just a few. Through these courses, we were able to discover talented individuals within our own organization who could step up to leadership roles when they became available. I would always recommend that our team members engage in continuing education—and one employee in particular recommended the same to me: "So, Leo, what classes are *you* taking?"

It was a great question, so I challenged myself to keep learning. I consulted with Marty O'Neill, who suggested the Harvard Business School's Owner/President Management Program (OPM), which is considered the gold standard among executive education programs. The OPM program provides three years of immersion training from Harvard Business School's finest faculty, and I ultimately graduated from the program in 2010. This was important to me, not only to continue enhancing my own knowledge, but also to set an example for the company—to show that leadership wasn't above taking the recommendations we handed out.

Early on in Tenacity Solutions' history I had several epiphanies about the way in which we were mentoring and checking in on employees—as well as how I was specifically interacting with them. My first epiphany was when I realized that I was spending about 80 percent of my time on squeaky wheels—on negative issues. This left me with no more than 20 percent of my time to go out and enable my employees to set the world on fire. The question that followed that was a simple one: *Why?*

My employees across the board clearly needed my attention and guidance—so why wasn't I giving them what they needed *before* the wheels started to squeak? To that end, I set about spending 80 percent of my time with the non-squeaky wheels, the employees that kept the organization moving forward and were most ready to set the world on fire. The other epiphany, and it should not come as a shocker to any new entrepreneur, was that I was spending too much of my time working in the company rather than on my company. Your organization will never fulfill its unique potential unless you focus your energies on your employees, enabling them to drive success with your organization's customers, partners, and investors.

At that point, I determined I would start visiting every one of my employees once a month, every month of the year. I didn't fully appreciate until later what it meant to these team members to have the company's CEO personally stop by. An unanticipated benefit of this was that customers were often in the vicinity when I made my visits, and this gave them the chance to see that Tenacity was a company in which the leadership interacted with the workforce. We were integrated; we were on the same page. These informal visits also frequently gave customers the opportunity to solicit insights directly from me. It was also a chance for the customers to highlight the outstanding work of those individuals in their areas.

One thing that gives employees the confidence they need is the understanding that they're not going to be reprimanded or lose their jobs if they make a mistake. When I mentored team members, spending this one-on-one time with them, I tried to instill in them the willingness to take chances and, if they failed, to "fail fast." We all make mistakes, so the best approach is to completely forego the worried hand-wringing. Learn all you can learn from your errors, then move on quickly.

At Tenacity, my commitment to being there for my employees went well beyond corporate retreats and even beyond the monthly personal visits. I wanted to be present for—and accountable to—

every individual. This meant I mentored new hires, acknowledged their accomplishments at monthly staff meetings and off-site, and

> *One thing that gives employees the confidence they need is the understanding that they're not going to be reprimanded or lose their jobs if they make a mistake.*

also sat in on every termination. Sadly, it isn't always fun and games. Sometimes, employees are not the right fit for your organization, and as the leader you must be present when those decisions are made and executed. This, too, is an opportunity to build commitment to the organization by showing your leadership team you are at their side not only when things are going well, but when tough decisions have to be made and carried out.

In addition, my office had an open-door policy. I imposed no restrictions on the subject matter or tone of employee visits. Sometimes, people stopped by to formally discuss a serious matter with me, with the aim of working together to mastermind a solution. Other times, to put it frankly, they just needed to bitch.

And hey, I understood that there was a need for both types of meetings every so often; I just needed to make sure I understood what the goal of the meeting was early on so I could adapt. When certain employees I'd come to know fairly well would stop by, I'd cut right to the chase and ask them, "Are we strategizing today, or is this a bitch session?" And if it was the latter, so be it.

I made it a priority to stay so well connected with the Tenacity team that when we held our annual Christmas party, I knew our employees *and* their significant others and their kids by name. Prior to these events my assistant would show me pictures of the staff and their family members and quiz me to keep me sharp. Acknowledging the contributions that significant others make to your organization is paramount. Their well-being directly affects their significant other's work output, quality, and dedication to the company.

Employee engagement isn't something you can fake, and you won't see any benefits from it if you're just doing it sporadically, treating it as a last-minute thought or a necessary burden. When you enthusiastically engage with your team—giving them regular evidence of your accessibility, learning their names, and acknowledging the importance of their lives outside of work—you encourage them to feel they have a personal stake in the company. When you foster a sense of personal connection between you and your employees, a connection is likely to form in turn between the employees and the business itself. And that connection is invaluable to your team's productivity and loyalty.

> *Employee engagement isn't something you can fake, and you won't see any benefits from it if you're just doing it sporadically, treating it as a last-minute thought or a necessary burden.*

BUSINESS LESSONS FROM THE AVIATION WORLD

DAVE HARTMAN, PRESIDENT,
HARTMAN EXECUTIVE ADVISORS

"Flight, [this is] Sonar, we have contact on a Soviet Victor submarine, bearing two-seven-zero degrees, range two miles, estimated depth two hundred feet."

For the first nine years of my working life, I had the pleasure of serving as a naval flight officer/aircraft mission commander on board the P-3C Orion for the US Navy. Those years were among the proudest of my career, and even before I resigned my commission as a US naval officer, they led me into my second career in business and information technology.

The navy was fertile training ground, and not surprisingly I've taken many of the leadership lessons and philosophies learned there into each of my roles since. However, I couldn't have predicted the impact these lessons would have on my current role as president of Hartman Executive Advisors.

Following are five key lessons I learned as an aircraft mission commander—lessons that have been invaluable to me as a business owner and strategic technology advisor.

1. Constantly scan your instruments and surroundings.

Pilots learn to keep a constant rotating scan of their primary cockpit instruments (airspeed, direction, altitude, attitude) and of the surrounding environment outside. This cockpit scan of key data is critical to flight safety and efficiency.

On one particular flight I'll never forget, I noticed that one of our pilots had obviously become distracted and wasn't going through his normal scan. It turned out that he was getting married in a few weeks; his mind was probably elsewhere. In any case, it was around dusk, and without the inside cabin lights on, he couldn't possibly see his instruments. Because it was a training flight, we simply watched him to see how long it would take him to realize his error. He just kept staring out the windshield instead of noticing anything was wrong.

As business leaders, how often do we get locked in on a particular metric and forget the other critical metrics around us?

At our company, we train our CIOs to maintain a constant scan of key strategic, tactical, and even operational metrics, but also to occasionally poke their heads outside the department and even the company to understand how the world out there is changing. The same is true for CEOs—though strategic business leaders likely need to spend even more time outside the four walls of their offices. However, we can't ever forget to keep a constant scan of key "dashboard" metrics inside our "cockpits."

2. You're only as good as the team supporting you.

As I've said, as a naval flight officer and mission commander, I had the privilege of flying the P-3C Orion—the Sub Hunter, as it was called. The thirteen members of my crew were among the best air crewmen in the navy, and we were often called on for challenging or critical missions.

None of what we accomplished would have been possible without a great crew working together. I may have been the senior officer, but I knew that without guys like Petty Officers Jones and Jackson, we wouldn't have been nearly as effective. Even F-A18 fighter jet pilots, who fly solo in their cockpits, aren't really flying solo. They need to rely on their ground crew, maintenance crews, wingmen, and even air traffic control to accomplish their missions and return home safely.

There's an old expression in business that no one is an island. Great companies build great teams, encourage teamwork, and discourage "heroism." Solo efforts that are more about one person's capabilities, accomplishments, or talents—rather than the best interests of the team or company—tend to undermine the team and distract from the mission at hand.

Solo efforts that are more about one person's capabilities, accomplishments, or talents—rather than the best interests of the team or company—tend to undermine the team and distract from the mission at hand.

3. *Trust your instruments.*

Aviators learn to trust their instruments. In aviation, "false horizons" occur when various natural or geometric formations on the skyline disorient pilots from the actual horizon, prompting them to slowly descend when they believe they are in level flight. There have been documented cases of long flights over water, for instance, in which planes have crashed into the sea because of this phenomenon.

In the business world, we can become so focused on a particular metric that we see something that isn't there. We let intuition get in the way of sound, data-based decision-making. Good aviators learn to trust—and corroborate—their instruments in order to keep this from happening. The best business leaders I've worked with and followed over the years know that while intuition, knowledge, and experience are important, backing up your decisions with sound, fact-based data is critical.

A client of ours learned that firsthand. This was a community bank whose revenue depended predominantly on agriculture clients. As the bank grew, however, the seasonality of the farming industry began to negatively affect cash flow. Knowing their customers, the executive team made a few assumptions about which related rural-client segments might hold the key to diversification for them.

We convinced them to allow us to analyze their clients and profitability, and what we found shocked them; their most profitable and loyal clients were actually small medical practices. Armed with this new information, they developed a strategy focused on growing this client segment, which had a tremendous influence on the seasonality of their cash flow and the diversification of their client base.

4. Checklists save lives!

Remember the incredible story of Captain Chesley "Sully" Sullenberger, who crash-landed US Airways Flight 1549 safely into New York's Hudson River in January 2009? Even amid chaotic conditions, in an emergency for which one couldn't possibly train or prepare, Sully and his copilot went right to their emergency procedures checklists and miraculously performed an unprecedented water landing with zero loss of life.

Even though most pilots and aviators know their procedures by heart—takeoff procedures, landing procedures, engine-start procedures, and emergency procedures—they always pull out their checklists to ensure that they don't miss a critical step. Training, knowledge of procedures, and meticulous preparation can enable us to do extraordinary things.

The same can and should be true in business. Now, I'm not expecting us to pull out a checklist every time we onboard a new employee or sign up a new client—the stakes aren't typically life or death—but standardized and effective procedures can make the difference between success and mistakes leading to unrecognized failures. Especially in a crisis, our ability to lean on known and practiced procedures can mean the difference between rapid recovery and years of unintended and unwanted ripple effects.

Cybersecurity is a central issue discussed in boardrooms and executive suites all over the country today. Businesses are spending tens and hundreds of thousands of dollars on monitoring systems, firewalls, and detection systems.

But have they developed, practiced, and communicated disaster recovery and business continuity procedures that will ensure rapid recovery in the event of a crisis? Have they developed an effective incident response plan? What happens in the minutes immediately following the discovery of

Especially in a crisis, our ability to lean on known and practiced procedures can mean the difference between rapid recovery and years of unintended and unwanted ripple effects.

a breach? Who is notified? Who speaks for the company if the press gets involved? Is there adequate legal and insurance representation? The minutes and hours after crisis strikes are not the time to decide on and implement response procedures. Just ask the executives at Target, Sony, or Equifax.

"Practice doesn't make perfect; *perfect* practice makes perfect." This was a favorite saying of one of my first flight instructors. Take practice seriously; don't just go through the motions. Think about how you'll react when the time comes for action. Put yourself in the seat of your clients, your employees, and even your competitors. As a leader, do what you can to make "practice" as real as possible. Aboard the P-3, we got to do our mission every day for real—which made for a much more intense operating environment.

My flight instructor's words never meant more to me than during one particular flight over the Mediterranean Sea in the early 1990s. Our mission was to find a Soviet nuclear submarine that intel said was in the region. Suddenly, a hit on sonar indicated she was nearby. For the next four hours, our crew tracked her through changes in speed and depth and various other maneuvers the Soviet sub captain employed as he attempted to lose us. This particular sub was one of the newest and quietest in the Soviet fleet, and it was critical that we not lose contact. He never did lose us, and we were able to successfully hand off contact to the next crew before returning to base.

In that situation, we didn't have time to think about how to react or come up with a strategy on the spot. We had to rely on our training, our procedures, and the confidence each of us had in the others to do the job without error.

Ironically, a few months earlier our crew had been part of an annual training exercise in which we were tasked with finding and tracking one of the US Navy's quietest nuclear submarines. We located her and tracked her for several hours through a dizzying array of maneuvers and tactics that tested our training. After the flight, the US sub captain sent a letter to the admiral in charge of Naval Aviation Atlantic, praising the efforts of our crew and saying that ours was the first P-3 aircrew ever to track his submarine in that manner. I was certain that without this training, our rendezvous with the Soviet sub wouldn't have turned out as it did.

5. Include an alternate landing site in your flight plan.

Whether you are flying an airplane or growing a business, establishing an ultimate destination (business goals, project goals, or personal growth goals) is critical, but so is having a solid plan B. Pilots can't even file their flight plans without designating an alternate airfield, and because business and life rarely go as planned, neither should we as business leaders. As the saying goes, you get what you measure. At Hartman, we have repeatedly seen that when we establish goals for ourselves—or our clients—and commit them to writing, they happen. Perhaps not exactly as we intended, but they happen.

Successful alternate flight plans require two components. First, they need to be created with forethought and intention; you shouldn't just pick a random airfield near your destination. Second, you need to be able to recognize quickly when it's necessary to change your heading toward your alternate—your plan B.

> *Whether you are flying an airplane or growing a business, establishing an ultimate destination (business goals, project goals, or personal growth goals) is critical, but so is having a solid plan B.*

The most effective alternate airfield is one that can be reached efficiently but isn't so close to the original destination that you may encounter the same problems that are affecting your first choice (weather, for instance). The same is true for your business. If you needed to execute your plan B, would it represent somewhere you really wanted to land? Would it constitute an actual desired destination, or was it just chosen so you would *have* a plan B—so you could put a check in that box?

Most importantly, know when it is time to turn toward the alternate landing site. Aviators use the term *point of no return* to designate the point at which fuel is insufficient to safely return to base. According to the *Merriam-Webster Unabridged* dictionary, it's also "a critical point [as in development or a course of action] at which turning back or reversal is not possible." The question is, do we recognize that point before we pass it? Or are we so committed to a project, plan, or colleague that we fail to recognize when success is no longer an option?

* * *

As I reflect on the experiences that have shaped my career, the honor of flying for the US Navy and the opportunity to lead my own business have certainly been the highlights. People have often commented that it must have been risky to start a business from nothing while raising my family—and I'm sure some would see flying airplanes as a risky lifestyle as well.

But I actually see myself as a *measured* risk taker. As we've grown Hartman Executive Advisors, there have certainly been risks, bumps, and stumbles along the way—but adhering to the principles and disciplines outlined here has enabled us to mitigate much of the risk inherent in growth. As a result, we have been able to remain focused on—and achieve—our objective of becoming the nation's leading strategic technology leadership and advisory firm.

TROUBLESOME CONVERSATIONS: TRANSFORMING DIFFICULTY INTO POSSIBILITY

STAN SACK, PhD, ORGANIZATIONAL PSYCHOLOGIST AT PERSONA, INC.

Let's say that team member M, who has three years of tenure, wants to meet with you to discuss her annual review. It invariably falls three months after her anniversary date. Her hire date was in the final month of your fiscal year—just before the books close and travel time begins. She's aware that other team members receive their annual reviews within weeks of their hire dates.

From your perspective, as company leader, the reason for the anomaly in her review time is simple. But does this translate into an easy, stress-free conversation with her? Hardly.

Whether you fully understand why you're dreading a conversation such as this one or not, you may find yourself wanting to procrastinate. The urge is to keep rescheduling meetings with her at the last minute so you don't become mired in a troublesome talk.

This chapter looks at why we, as business owners and managers, tend to avoid conversations like this one, how this makes matters worse, and what we can do to alleviate the common pains involved in discussing such matters. At the end of the chapter, we'll return to this example in order to compare right and wrong ways of handling this difficult conversation.

Like a tightrope act above a tiger's cage, difficult conversations can trigger fear of heights (anxiety over the high stakes involved), fear of falling (worry over losing control, being criticized, or looking weak in the eyes of a team member), and, in some extreme cases, fear of being eaten alive (fear that you'll get stuck in a point–counterpoint argument that reaches no conclusion but instead "eats up" your time, resources, and patience). When you consider the difficult conversation's similarities to walking a rope only feet above restless tigers, it's easy to grasp why so many people dread the prospect.

Before we address how to combat the problem, let's look at those characteristics that comprise a difficult conversation.

At the simplest level, these are discourses in which one person presents a point and another person offers a counterpoint. Of course, many types of discussions launch from that same basic setup without becoming contentious or making either party uncomfortable— difficult discussions are about more than just disagreeing.

During the difficult interactions we're talking about here, you'll hear sentences that start, "Yes, but … " This is an indication that neither party is really listening to the other. What they're typically doing instead of listening is waiting in silence for their own turn to talk. Perhaps the most prominent feature of a difficult discussion is that the parties are focused on achieving agreement—not *alignment*.

Often we enter into these exchanges with the goal of proving we're right—and getting the other party to agree. It's an attitude that blocks us from conceding that the other party has a good point about anything, and, accordingly, it brings true communication to a standstill.

When this happens, the biggest loser is your company. Why? Because troublesome conversations contain possibilities and solutions that never get identified because each party is (a) focused on making their own point and (b) easily distracted—losing mindfulness and presence in the conversation.

Perhaps the most prominent feature of a difficult discussion is that the parties are focused on achieving agreement—not alignment.

Ending in perfect consensus is not a requirement of successful discussions. However, you do need to reach a point where you and the other party respectfully consent to act based on a certain decision. This isn't agreement, but is alignment—which should be the goal.

It's Not About Who Is Right

Have you ever walked away from a conversation feeling completely drained? If you have, chances are you got so caught up in the outcome of the interaction that it ceased to be a conversation at all. We tend to fail equally on the fronts of listening and meaningfully contributing when we're honed in on being right—avoiding being wrong, trying not to look bad, dodging the answer "no." This can happen to anyone, but it's especially detrimental when you're the boss and you connect with employees in this way.

Conversations that center on who's right create barriers to listening and thus limit your opportunity to recognize new solutions. When you, as a leader, initiate interactions of this variety with your supervisees, you discourage them from contributing. However inadvertently, you can come across as inflexible and wind up invalidating the other person.

Avoidance and Negativity: Problems with the Most Common Responses

What do we, as business leaders, do when the prospect of a difficult conversation triggers negative emotion? As mentioned in the example that begins this chapter, we tend to procrastinate. For the sake of temporary relief, we dismiss or delay the conversation, either through apparent stalling tactics or simply by acting unapproachable, making ourselves a little less accessible to the individual we're putting off dealing with.

> **We tend to fail equally on the fronts of listening and meaningfully contributing when we're honed in on being right—avoiding being wrong, trying not to look bad, dodging the answer "no."**

Clearly, this does not make the problem go away.

Even if you avoid the conversation effectively enough that the other party stops seeking a meeting—your opportunity cost will be huge. A team member who needs to speak with you but is put off can take it personally and grow resentful. The individual may then discuss the situation with others to gain support for their increasingly negative view of you.

If you're not directly avoiding the person but also not engaging them, you may well develop a negative attitude toward them. This can manifest as taking a belittling or dismissive stance with them, or the topic they wish to discuss, during group meetings. If you act this way, it's about more than simple pettiness—you're probably, subconsciously, trying to make the relationship so unpleasant that the other person withdraws their request to hash things out. And maybe, even better, they'll learn to keep discomforting problems to themselves and not burden you with them at all. But even if you achieve that, and the temporary relief that comes with it, then you're stuck with your means of accomplishing it: a now-poisoned relationship between you and the other party.

It's easy to see the heavy toll of avoidance and negativity. Your overall cost here can include lost opportunities to improve efficiencies, loss of team member commitment, and costs associated with high employee turnover, such as recruiting fees, onboarding, ramping up to full productivity, etc.

When you take the tack of negativity, you risk escalating the conflict, as back-channel support groups form among coworkers who share views similar to those of the other party. As with straightforward avoidance, when you react negatively, you lose opportunities to solve matters efficiently and thus reduce expenses. An opportunity cost of this method is that your company can wind up with a lot of job dissatisfaction and turnover.

The Doom Loop of "Filters"

We all tend to bring filters to our interactions with others, the filters through which we interpret difficult conversations cause misperception and mutual mystification. They hamper our ability to understand the meaning behind the actual words being spoken. When these filters are applied, our communication suffers frequent gaps between what was heard by the listener and what was meant by the speaker.

We're applying filters when we jump to or overreach for conclusions. A truly harmful filter is the idea that for one party to be right, the other has to be wrong—and that there's no being partially right or wrong. The all-or-nothing filter has waylaid many otherwise productive discussions, as it opens the door to needless competition for who's the *most right.*

A Parable on Filters

Let's say you and two other people are having dinner in a restaurant. You end up getting bad service, which makes the evening unpleasant for everyone. As your table discusses this poor service, your dinner companion to your right proposes that the waitstaff may be shorthanded tonight or busier than they had expected. The person to your left suggests that the kitchen could be slow tonight for reasons beyond the waitstaff's control. But you offer a third possible explanation: the waiter overheard a comment you made about the restaurant and consequently has been delivering inadequate service on purpose.

> A truly harmful filter is the idea that for one party to be right, the other has to be wrong— and that there's no being partially right or wrong.

If you believe your own explanation—bad service due to the waiter not liking your group based on the overheard comment—you may end up (a) making a complaint to the manager or host station and/or (b) recommending little or no tip. Meanwhile, your companions, who don't buy into your point of view, just feel sorry for the waiter.

All three of you witnessed poor service. That's objective data. But once you associated the data with an interpretation—"the waiter doesn't like us"—then your feelings and actions became driven not by objective data but by *your interpretation* of the data. This is automatic, and it occurs in every interpersonal transaction.

It's a deal killer—and an expense creator.

Transformative Opportunities Open a World of Possibilities

Instead of viewing an employee's request to meet with you as a warning that difficulty lies ahead, try seeing it as an opportunity—not only to resolve the specific issue at hand, but also to improve your communication and comfort level with the other party.

Transforming what you once thought of as a difficult conversation into a "possibilities" discussion requires that you change your paradigm of thinking about the other party or the topic involved. Specifically, you must shift away from your concerns about being right and being seen as tough; you need to stop worrying so much that if you give in on any issue, you will be in the wrong and therefore look weak.

In a conversation of possibilities, the focus is on understanding (not hammering home your own point) and problem-solving (not distancing yourself from the reality that a problem exists). The primary skills involved in this sort of conversation—namely listening and questioning—are competencies that fall under the umbrella of emotional intelligence (EQ). And central to EQ is strong self-awareness.

To remain self-aware throughout a conversation, you need to continually monitor your verbal and nonverbal messages, emotions, and tone. Most of us know to remain mindful of the message we're delivering; when we harness our EQ, we're also mindful of the way we're delivering this message.

When you put in the necessary work to remain self-aware, you will come across as authentic. To understand just how important this is, consider how discussions will go if you don't seem genuine—you will seem, instead, artificial and even patronizing. This will put up a barricade between you and the other party and prevent you from understanding their point of view.

Beyond working on your self-awareness and shifting your mental paradigm, the biggest transformative step you will take is starting with a firm agenda. This means you don't jump in with your point right away—you establish the parameters of what is it be discussed, making sure you're both in agreement. A meeting that proceeds without a firm agenda is destined to waste your time and end not only with no solutions but possibly with more problems than you originally had!

> *When you put in the necessary work to remain self-aware, you will come across as authentic.*

A meeting with no agenda, or even a loose agenda, is a boat adrift on stormy seas. An *explicit, agreed-upon agenda* is your navigation system—it helps you stay within the necessary context. Look at the context itself as your rudder. Many troublesome, difficult conversations fail because the parties go off course into other topics. Keep the follow equation in mind for a successful possibilities conversation.

Agenda + Context = Navigation + Rudder

When the agenda is clear and agreed upon, the parties involved don't get lost along the way, and they don't build up resistance toward each other. This means you never reach a stalemate and feel the need to table to table the conversation, which would only encourage you to dread and avoid it all over again. Instead, you redirect to your explicit agenda as needed. If off-agenda divergent topics do surface, you can prevent them from taking over by scheduling a discussion of those topics for another time.

Throughout the discussion, recognize the buy-in is incremental and requires that you continually achieve alignment. Gaining that alignment at the beginning won't help much if you don't make efforts to the earn the person's buy-in at subsequent steps.

When you remain reflective and evaluative, rather than judgmental and dismissive, you're practicing the art and science of discovery. Simply put, you're asking the right questions to get to the bottom of the real problem. You'll hear yourself using phrases such as "Let me tell you what I hear you saying" or "Tell me what you're hearing me say."

In the following pages, you find a table that helps break down and summarize much of in information presented in this chapter. Before we go on to that, I'd like, one last time, to emphasize the most important concept in "possibilities conversations": alignment.

When you've made the effort to remain self-aware, reflective, and collaborative throughout a discussion, you'll find that reaching alignment comes much more easily. It's a good indication you're on the right path when you're using phrases such as "I know you won't like this, and I respect that" and "I hear your perspective, and here's the point where we need to align."

As you train yourself to stay away from the bad habits frequently triggered by difficult discussions, keep your end goal in mind. The other party does not need to fully appreciate your proposed solution and you don't need to be in 100 percent agreement with them. The important thing is that you work together to reach a point of alignment so that action can be taken and you can both move onward.

Point–Counterpoint Encounter *(Activity)*	The meeting starts on time. **Leader:** M, I understand you want to talk to me about your performance reviews. What's on your mind?
Takeaway/What Is Achieved *(Do these actions produce the right outcomes to achieve the desired result?)*	• No agenda is set for the meeting. • First step of buy-in/alignment is missed.
Affirmation–Confirmation Encounter *(Activity)*	**Leader:** M, making sure we're both on the same page, let me take a moment and confirm the agenda for our meeting. We're here to discuss your concerns about your performance reviews—is that right? **M:** Yes, the timing of my reviews specifically." **Leader:** "Good. Now just to confirm, our meeting is scheduled until 2 p.m. Is that what you have on your calendar? I can tell this is very important to you, and it should be. Why don't you start so I can understand your concerns.
Takeaway/What Is Achieved *(Do these actions produce the right outcomes to achieve the desired result?)*	• Agreeing on the agenda and time for the meeting is the first step of buy-in and will lead to collaboration. • The Leader remains in control, using the agenda and time for meeting. Leader is affirming, supportive, and open.

Point-Counterpoint Encounter *(Activity)*	**M:** I really don't understand why it takes you three months to meet with me to review my contributions for the year. I've been here three years, and my review is late every time. It's not that way for everyone else—I know; I checked.
Takeaway/What Is Achieved *(Do these actions produce the right outcomes to achieve the desired result?)*	The overt or declared problem
Affirmation-Confirmation Encounter *(Activity)*	**Leader:** Tell me more about this because it sounds like you've been upset for quite a while. Have you talked to anyone in HR? You are right to be concerned. I checked, and everyone on the team is reviewed within thirty days of their anniversary. Waiting three months without an explanation sends an unfortunate message. I can understand
Takeaway/What Is Achieved *(Do these actions produce the right outcomes to achieve the desired result?)*	• Discovery and affirmation • Asking questions and affirming • Helping M fully express her concerns

Point-Counterpoint Encounter *(Activity)*	**Leader:** I don't understand your concern. We have our review every year—we never miss it. You get a merit increase and we backdate it.
Takeaway/What Is Achieved *(Do these actions produce the right outcomes to achieve the desired result?)*	The true concern is dismissed.
Affirmation-Confirmation Encounter *(Activity)*	**Leader:** M, let me summarize the problem as I'm hearing it. …. And because of this, you feel that I/we do not value you or the work that you are doing because this happens over and over. Do I understand your concerns correctly?
Takeaway/What Is Achieved *(Do these actions produce the right outcomes to achieve the desired result?)*	• Validation of the problem without judgment • M feels relieved that someone actually is LISTENING

Point-Counterpoint Encounter *(Activity)*	**M:** Why am I the only one who has to wait three months? If you don't want me here, why not just tell me?
Takeaway/What Is Achieved *(Do these actions produce the right outcomes to achieve the desired result?)*	M feels unheard and undervalued.
Affirmation-Confirmation Encounter *(Activity)*	**Leader:** You asked why you're the exception having to wait—correct? **M:** Yes, it's only me who waits, and that's not fair. **Leader:** Of course it's not fair. Let's understand the reason. It turns out that using the anniversary date as the time for the review has been our policy. The hire dates of everyone else fall in the second or third quarter. You are the only team member whose hire date falls in the latter part of Q4. That's the problem. The policy did not take that into account. Make sense? **M:** Well, I shouldn't have to suffer the consequence of some policy that doesn't fit me, or you should have brought me on in the new quarter. **Leader:** I see that.
Takeaway/What Is Achieved *(Do these actions produce the right outcomes to achieve the desired result?)*	• Accepting: not debating or minimizing • Checking in with M to confirm she understands. • "I see that" neither confirms nor debates M's statement.

SELLING YOUR BUSINESS MADE SIMPLE

MICHAEL MERCURIO, PRINCIPAL,
OFFIT KURMAN, P.A.

For those who haven't previously sold a business—and that's most people—the process can be daunting. As principal and chair of the Business Law and Transactions Practice Group at Offit Kurman, I have helped countless entrepreneurs—on both the sell side and the buy side—to navigate the transaction with ease. I've found the infographics presented here to be powerful in breaking everything down into simple phases. This explains who will be involved and what you need to think about at each step along the way.

My first infographic, the "Business Combination Tornado," translates the entire process into clear, easy-to-grasp steps. The funnel design helps illustrate how close you are—as a seller or buyer—to your final objective at any given point.

ANATOMY OF THE DEAL:
The Business Combination Tornado

BUYER

Market analysis and target(s) identification

Financing and capital needs

Indications of interest and preliminary diligence

SELLER

Determination to sell, valuation; hiring of advisors

Putting together the "book" and getting to market

Confidentiality and IOI analysis

Letter of Intent

Due Diligence, Financial, Legal, Operational

Contract Negotiation; Execution

Key Employee Discussions

Conduct Interviews and Consents

Closing; Public Announcements

Integration

The sum is greater than the parts

For questions or more information, please call Michael N. Mercurio at (301) 575-0332.

Offit|Kurman
Attorneys At Law
Trust Knowledge Confidence

Player Involvement per Phase

	Pre transaction Planning	Phase I: Letter of Intent	Phase II: Due Diligence	Phase III: Contracts	Phase IV: Closing	Phase V: Post Closing	Post transaction Planning
Seller	High	High	High	High	High	High	High
Buyer		High	High	High	High	High	High
M&A Consultant	Building	High	High	Half Phase Trailing			
Attorney	High	Building	High	High	High	High	High
Accountant	Building	High	High	Half Phase Trailing		Half Phase Trailing	Building
Financial Planner						Half Phase Building	
Business/ Life Coach	High						High
Phase Rule:	Find and eliminate skeletons; Create multiple options	Get exclusivity and keep flexibility with payments and pricing	Know what you want and get it in writing as the LOI may be your high water mark	Disclosure is your friend	Time is your enemy	Remember to dot the i's and cross the t's	Enjoy your new status in life; Make sure that you have considered life without the business.

Sell-Side M&A: Three Rules of Thumb for the Transaction

Rule #1: You Have Not Sold your Business until You Have Sold your Business

Rule #2: Get your Money Upfront - As Soon and as Much as Possible

Rule #3: Reduce and Eliminate your Trailing Liabilities

Level of Involvement

- Low
- High
- Building
- Half Phase Trailing
- Half Phase Building

Offit | Kurman
Attorneys At Law

For questions or more information, please call Michael N. Mercurio at (301) 575-0332.

If you've decided to sell and your company is large enough, you will likely turn to an investment banker; if the company is smaller and a little less sophisticated, you may use a business broker. Both of these could be considered M&A consultants. Someone who works exclusively in consultation could also fill that role. These are all people who can help company owners efficiently launch the transaction.

On the front side, what happens is this: You decide you want to sell your business, you go to an investment banker or broker, and they help evaluate the business. After assisting you in cleaning up and correctly posturing your company, they'll help market it.

Simply put, the M&A consultants work on the front end. They get you *to* the deal. They're very involved on the marketing side, from conducting interviews to analyzing the market to sending out marketing books that contain financials, history, proof of ownership, and so on for potential buyers to consider.

> **Simply put, the M&A consultants work on the front end. They get you to the deal.**

If all goes well, they'll see you through the point where interested parties start rolling in and you begin receiving letters of intent (LOIs). Once you have one or more LOIs, the work starts to fall more squarely on the shoulders of your attorney.

As lawyers, we also aid in tidying up and posturing the business, as M&A consultants do, but from there we're with the seller through every phase. Beyond negotiating LOIs and writing the contract itself, attorneys review with diligence, and we get the seller to closing and beyond—estate planning, asset protection, and so forth.

To delve into some of the finer points of the "Sell-Side Perspective" infographic, you'll notice my first rule of thumb for the transaction says, "You have not sold your business until you've sold your business."

It's important for both buyers and sellers to not act as though the sale is complete before every aspect of the transaction has been checked off—closing deliverables exchanged, necessary payments received, and so on. For sellers, this is particularly important. Even if you've signed the contract, had detailed discussions with the buyer, and are moving swiftly toward the close, the business is still yours.

What often happens is that sellers get caught up in the belief that the sale is a foregone conclusion—the business being as good as gone—so they take their eyes off the ball with respect to ongoing operations. For a couple of reasons, it's important to act, throughout all negotiations, as though you're not selling. The first is simply that you don't want the potential buyer seeing slip-ups.

You also need to consider that, for whatever reason, the deal may not close. And if doesn't, you're going to need to move forward with your business.

To give an example, I had a client some years back who was selling his plumbing business to a Japanese company that was doing a roll-up of contractors in the United States. We were about two weeks from closing when a tsunami hit Japan, wiping out one of the buyer's facilities—and prompting them to pull out of the deal. Unbeknown to me, my client had started living his post-business life and had essentially begun mailing it in. Because he let up in that way, he eventually went bankrupt.

You haven't sold your home until you hand over the keys. The same concept applies to your business. It's not actually done until it's done; that's a very simple statement with potentially drastic ramifications if you don't follow through.

> You haven't sold your home until you hand over the keys. The same concept applies to your business.

One important area this infographic also touches on is pretransaction planning. To illustrate this point, I would again call on the example of selling your home. Before you go to market, or before you even have a real estate agent take pictures, you may need to dress the place up a bit. Freshen the paint, change the carpets, fix the squeaky tap—those kinds of things.

Similarly, while your business may be able to sell as is, most buyers find they can optimize their value by carefully assessing their business and making sure they have all their ducks in a row. This can mean ensuring you don't have unfinished business or making sure that if there are contracts you never followed up with the vendor on and had them sign page 2—you go ahead and follow up.

Let's now look at what happens when you've worked with your M&A consultant and attorney, you've enticingly marketed your business, and you have received a letter of intent. What does this mean, in practical terms? An LOI is essentially a term sheet. It indicates how the buyer sees the transaction going, and it covers who the buyer is, how the proposed transaction structure might look, and any other terms and conditions the buyer might put into the agreement.

Usually the LOI includes the buyer's indication value and/or formulation of how that value is going to be paid. If they're going to pay you $1 million, the LOI spells out how exactly you're going to receive that million.

Buyers typically want two things when writing a letter of intent: flexibility (they'll try to not commit to heavy terms) and exclusivity. There can be some hurdles to clear in this area, because while buyers want to keep it flexible, sellers want specificity. Naturally sellers want to understand *exactly* what they're getting. The seller wants to know what cards the buyer's holding, but the buyer doesn't want to show them.

Exclusivity can also be a sticky topic for sellers, as this constitutes a window of time—perhaps thirty or sixty days—when they can deal only with the buyer. This is a period of commitment designated for getting the transaction accomplished. Any other parties the investment banker may have contacted, any others who may have had interest, are now frozen out. For a seller who has plenty of suitors, going exclusive can be a risky proposition.

This is one reason why, if the seller does deem it worthwhile to grant exclusivity and proceed with buyer A, the seller wants to push for the most favorable terms possible in the LOI.

From this point on, the buyer begins doing their diligence, verifying the seller's purchases, transaction structure, and so on. The buyer may find that things are in even better shape than they had anticipated. While that has been known to happen on occasion, I have never known of a buyer to say, "You know, I was going to pay you a million dollars, but your business is doing so wonderfully that now I'm going to pay you two million." In reality, buyers keep quiet and bask in the excellent deal they've found.

On the opposite side, the buyer's diligence could turn up factors that negatively impact the business. At that point, the buyer will want to change their terms. Typically, letters of intent aren't binding, so neither party is obligated to follow through with the transaction. The only binding aspects at this point are exclusivity and certain legal parameters, such as choice of law office.

There's an element that should be kept in mind at every phase throughout the process—from marketing to reviewing the LOI to diligence—and that's timing. For a seller, time is the enemy. That's listed as the rule of Phase IV: Closing. And there are a couple reasons this is true.

The first has to do with a certain air of confidence. Most sellers don't tell people they're selling. They don't tell their employees. They don't tell their customers. But the

> *For a seller, time is the enemy.*

longer a deal drags on, the likelier it is for the information to leak. If the news that you're selling gets to the market, and to your workforce, it can undercut the confidence placed in your business.

A point discussed previously applies here as well—don't forget that you're still the one at the helm of your business. You don't want to slack off only to find yourself without a successful sale and stuck with a now-suffering operation. You don't want to risk alienating your staff and customer base in case, again, the sale doesn't go as planned and you find yourself needing to count on them.

There are other reasons it's vital to move through this transaction as swiftly as possible while still ensuring each step is handled correctly. The longer a deal goes on, the more it costs the seller. The quicker you can get the deal finished and neatly packaged up, the better.

I'd also like to touch on the phase rule for Posttransactional Planning—to enjoy your new status in life. While that may not seem like traditional counsel for selling a business, I've seen many would-be sellers impeded from actually going through with the transaction because they haven't done much else with their lives—they've run their businesses. That's what they know.

When your business is your identity—your alter ego—it makes sense that you would have a hard time selling it; the looming need to adapt to a completely different lifestyle can be intimidating. Someone can sell a business, make a bunch of money—many millions even—and still feel unhappy. This is a predictable enough scenario when someone hasn't cultivated outside interests and hobbies. So, make sure you give yourself the chance to relax and explore new horizons.

A final note about working with your attorney. While it's understood that lawyers essentially manage risk for our clients, there's another level. At the front end, we determine what the client's objectives are and what risks the client cares about. This plays into how we negotiate provisions and terms in the contract. If the client doesn't care about a certain risk, it's not one we're going to focus on. On the other side, if the client feels strongly about a certain risk, we're going to do all we can to mitigate and minimize that risk.

This is an important distinction. For the most part, entrepreneurs are viewed as existing on the left side of the continuum, while attorneys live on the right side. Risk is part and parcel of being an entrepreneur; you're not going to grow your business without it. Attorneys, on the other hand, are in the business of not only *not* taking risks, but also making every effort to identify and eliminate them.

With this substantial gap between the two mindsets, there are many attorneys who will tell an entrepreneur selling a business, "I can't let you sign that deal," or, "You can't go forward with this agreement." But that's the wrong approach.

> *Risk is part and parcel of being an entrepreneur; you're not going to grow your business without it.*

This is where it's important, as a lawyer, to be mindful of any misalignment of objectives. We're there to help our clients' goals and desires come to fruition in a way that's smoothest and most productive. To achieve that, we need to make sure we're not projecting our own risk profile too much. That we're remembering who we're there to serve. It's like I always remind myself: I don't work for the transaction—I work for the client.

I WANT TO INSPIRE
AND BE INSPIRED

RHONDA CORNELSEN, FOUNDER,
HELM POINT SOLUTIONS

I started Helm Point Solutions in 2007—not *exactly* the best timing, considering the direction the economy was taking—to be a high-end software engineering company. It was meant to serve government and business clients by securing their data across a wide spectrum of the data-driven marketplace. Today, we have a team that is passionate about people and our customers' mission—and that's one of the reasons the company has thrived even in a bumpy economic climate. Another reason is that we work hard to inspire excellence in the people we work with. I highly value those moments when members of our team inspire me.

In 2008, we seized an opportunity to grow Helm Point by acquiring a smaller software engineering firm, Ward Solutions, which had about twenty existing contracts in place. In addition to software engineering, they had a physical security practice—a field we knew very little about at the time. But it came with the acquisition, so we decided to roll with it.

Over the last few years, potential clients and casual observers alike have wondered why any company would link these two specialties together. The answer is that with data hacks and physical threats becoming daily events, it occurred to us that there's a need to help people feel more secure.

Given the relative youth of our company, and our unbridled enthusiasm, luck was with us—and I do mean that there was not a *lot* of foresight involved. It's important to remember that all this took place before "active shooter" training became mandatory for your preschooler. Today, Helm Point has evolved into a team working to deter cyber- and physical-security threats for a wide spectrum of clients. In the cybersecurity realm, we help to harden clients' systems and preserve their critical, operational data. On the physical-security side, we offer planning and execution-of-force protection that helps our customers pursue their goals with a heightened sense of safety.

Our flexibility and eagerness to expand paid off. In 2009, Helm Point won a security contract based on our planning and marketing. Step by step, we've evolved to become what we are today, a company that excels in cybersecurity as well as physical security.

While a number of factors have contributed to our success in this competitive, continually evolving field—flexibility and subject-matter expertise among them—I think the number-one thing that defines us is our people. To me, the company is the team. That's no generalization—as anyone who knows me professionally will tell you. From the beginning of my time leading this company, my role has been to help team members find their passion. This drives not only the wide-reaching practices we implement but also what most people would consider the "small things."

When I shake someone's hand, I always try to assess what that person's really about. What are their values, their interests, their passions? I ask myself, "Could I work with someone like this? Is this someone who would help our company and our customers in their mission? Is this someone who could evolve with us?"

My success is working with our team to help them discover their *superpowers*. What is a superpower in this context? It's whatever you bring to the table that empowers and drives you. And while I personally enjoy helping people unearth that healthy spark within them, it makes a great deal of sense from a business perspective as well. Because the next question I ask is selfish: "How can we, as a company, *use* that superpower?"

It's also helpful to keep in mind that the reason for helping people identify their passions is to set them free—to do what they're best at doing. I reflect on a time when we had a VIP event at a customer's site. As people streamed in, I kept giving instructions to a team member who was new to Helm Point: "These are the tasks for today … here's what the customers are going to expect from you."

When I stopped obsessing, he looked at me and said, in a perfectly friendly way, "You know, I took care of a significant piece of the last presidential inauguration. I think I can handle these VIPs for you."

It was his polite way of saying: "Rhonda, I've got this. For me, this is just like putting my shoes on." This was, in other words, his superpower; it was why he'd joined the team in the first place.

It wasn't *my* superpower, though; I had to work hard to get the details of it right, so I defaulted to thinking that others needed all the same reminders and preparatory work. This was a key lesson for me. I had to remember to trust the top-shelf team I'd hired to do exactly what I'd hired them to do.

When you set out to build a team of people you trust to do high-level work, you look for those superpowers. You look for the willingness to evolve and pay attention to the details—and you also look for impressive insight. Those who offer it are people who will not only learn from you, but also teach you.

To ensure success as our team evolved, we needed them to understand that while we were a service company that dealt in cybersecurity and physical security, we were also in the business of customer service. Well, we came to a point in the company's growth that required us to hire someone to handle internal scheduling. I was looking at one woman in particular for the role, and in the course of our interview, she said to me, "Customer service is really important, but you have to understand that the ketchup isn't free."

> When you set out to build a team of people you trust to do high-level work, you look for those superpowers. You look for the willingness to evolve and pay attention to the details—and you also look for impressive insight.

That inspired me. In essence, she was saying that tossing ten packets of ketchup into the fast-food sandwich bag with the burger is a disservice to the customer—and the bottom line. Her insight was that you need to deliver excellent customer service; however, you will fail if you spend a month on software programming that needs to be delivered in a week, or spend an hour on the phone with a customer when you can answer their question in a minute or two.

I was blown away by her insight. She showed me, up front, that she had a balanced view of what the customer needed and what we needed as a company. Anyone who could teach me something in the course of a job interview—in a succinct, catchy way at that— would be a valuable addition to the team. So we hired her, and she quickly became part of our management team. The teams she leads are empowered to find solutions, and they have consistently met or exceed our customers' expectations.

Beyond developing an insightful team with the right perspectives in mind—and with their individual superpowers in place—I also see great value in cultivating a diverse team. We're fortunate at Helm Point that our team is diverse in a variety of ways—demographically, but also in terms of perspective, superpowers, interests, and more.

I remember one of my first managers telling me he preferred people who looked like him, thought like him, and had backgrounds and interests similar to his own. I also remember watching him fail—he couldn't appreciate the person who was his polar opposite.

I've found that an important extension of helping people find their superpowers is matching complementary folks together. At the same time, I like to make sure the people I match up in teams are able to appreciate one another's qualities. Sometimes software developers like to work with other software developers because they get them—they trust that skill set. I want them to be able to look at a teammate who knows zip about software and say, "Well, they're more creative. They don't think the way I do, but that's a good thing."

This is the kind of situation in which the importance of diversity in perspectives comes into play. If you're a big-picture thinker, someone who is able to focus on small but important details will act in a complementary role.

My mission and passion is to help the team use their amazing superpowers, to apply them to

If you're a big-picture thinker, someone who is able to focus on small but important details will act in a complementary role.

many diverse situations and create solutions for the customer. I also endeavor to help them see the superpowers of their teammates and understand how to call on their superpowers/passions when those powers will better serve the customer. One thing that initially surprised me was how unevenly our team's superpowers could sometimes be applied. I would often notice them choosing only certain times to pull out these powers.

Identifying this trend taught me that another part of my job as mentor is helping our team see the many opportunities they have to apply their unique skills. We all tend to get stuck in grooves in terms of how we use our abilities. That's where an outside perspective can be important. This can take the form of a manager or business leader saying to an employee, "I think you can apply your abilities from Project X to Project Y."

And the same is true for business leaders. Sometimes, we benefit richly from having an advisory board, another business leader, or a business consultant point out alternate ways for us to apply our strengths.

Our company is also generationally diverse. I think our oldest employee is just over eighty years of age, and our youngest is twenty. With generational diversity that widespread, you're naturally going to benefit from different perspectives and different attitudes that have been formed by different life experiences.

All those factors contribute to our identity as a team, and as a company. In a sense, we are a microcosm of the United States—a melting pot of ideas and perspectives, all of which we hope to optimize for the betterment of the company.

When the leadership of a company takes this approach of diligently creating a diverse, empowered team—and then showing its members how valuable they are to the company—it's natural that they will, in turn, show customers how valuable they are.

Some businesses consider customer service to be just doing what the customer asks them to do. But if you don't get in there—get your hands dirty and really seek to understand the customer's business—you're not doing your client base or yourself any favors. Your customer may or may not have a clear view of their ultimate, long-term needs; as a service provider, though, you need to have the clearest possible view of the precise need you're fulfilling. In this regard, software engineering is no different from carpet installation.

Consumer data is a big deal right now, as is trying to extract meaningful information from that data. Most companies have tons and tons of it being collected from every imaginable source, and while trying to extrapolate patterns from it to grow their business can be a challenge, it's also worthwhile. Why? Because that mountain of data contains your customers' explanations of exactly what they want and need.

My statistics teacher once said to me, "Statistics can show you anything. There's four out of five … " He loved mentioning that stat, four out of five, as in "Four out of five dentists surveyed recommend Crest." He would point to an example like that and ask, "Do you know what that means?"

I remained silent and waited for his explanation.

"We might've surveyed one thousand people and asked them about Crest. And if we lop off all of them but five, four out of five out of the thousand that we talked to recommended Crest," he'd finally explain. It doesn't tell you how many of the other 995 like Crest—it just says, "Four out of the five that we chose out of the sample liked Crest."

I think people today are picking up more and more on the artifice of the classic data interpretations like the four-out-of-five statistic. The result is an erosion of customer trust in a company and its products. In response, some people despair of extracting meaningful information—meaningful messages—from data.

I consider it worthwhile to learn which stats apply *accurately* to your industry—and which don't. Learn how to read between the lines of the numbers. Even better, work with an expert, someone for whom data interpretation is a superpower. Coordinate with that person to extract the core message being broadcast to you *by your own data.*

My main responsibility as a business leader is to inspire our employees. I want them to support our customers with efforts above and beyond what is expected. If I do this right, the ultimate effect of my work—helping our team members grasp and apply their superpowers—is that customers will have a firmer grasp on, and a more successful path to, their own goals.

> I believe businesses succeed when leaders empower employees to look beyond the task at hand and understand the big picture of what they're really accomplishing.

Finally, I believe businesses succeed when leaders empower employees to look beyond the task at hand and understand the big picture of what they're really accomplishing. This is the path that unlocks—in the systems or software engineer, the customer service representative, or the security specialist—the superhero. Only then will they inspire their managers, as mine inspire me.

A FOR-PROFIT MISSION

KRIS KURTENBACH, OWNER,
COLLABORATIVE COMMUNICATIONS

Before I became the founding partner and owner of
Collaborative Communications, a boutique firm specializing in
education and learning, I was trained in journalism and English lit-
erature. Right after leaving college, I held a variety of journalism-
related jobs: writing, editing, photo editing, and so on. I covered
education hearings for *Congressional Quarterly* and wrote about
education issues for its sister publication, *Governing* magazine. The
next step in marrying my interests in journalism and education, I
decided, was to attend graduate school.

After I graduated from the Harvard Graduate School of
Education, I ended up working at the US Department of Education,
where I helped write the policy that today is known as Title One.
After a short time there, however, I realized I was too removed from
what was happening on the ground. So I went to work for a nonprofit
that addressed how communities' education values affected the type
of schooling experience being provided to their kids.

That experience was important—I began to really understand

that it wasn't just a matter of communicating *to* people; it was about *two-way* communication. We needed to gain a true understanding of stakeholder opinions and belief systems, and then we could focus on public engagement. This strand of work involved not only community focus groups, but also community meetings and cross-sector community engagement.

However, after I left the Department of Education, and as I moved away from nonprofit education work and started working for communications consulting firms, I found that this notion of engagement I'd learned was not something most firms saw as profitable or practical. Because it wasn't boilerplate, it wasn't easily repeatable. Recognizing that engagement of this sort demanded certain skills and sensibilities that I had cultivated, I created my own firm.

Collaborative Communications was founded in 1999 as a for-profit company, and much like a law firm, it is organized into areas of practice. These areas include a spectrum of communications skill sets, services, and offerings. Digital services, for instance, encompasses web development, data visualizations, and the creation of simulations, games, and apps. This arena is all about helping people effectively portray themselves and engage with others electronically.

A second practice area is events and meetings management, which covers the soup-to-nuts work for meetings for thirty to three thousand attendees. In our media and engagement practice, we tackle what most people would categorize as PR work: messaging, strategic communications, positioning, partnerships, and social media activities. Our organizational learning practice looks not just at the communications work of organizations but at organizations as a whole. There we focus on business planning, coaching, and consulting—primarily with the executive directors and senior leadership of organizations.

Our work in education and learning extends to youth development and often includes efforts in community engagement and development. We predominantly work with foundations, large nonprofits, networks involved in school reform, community-based organizations, school districts, and state governments, and we provide an array of communications consulting services to advance their individual missions.

Additionally, we make a point of catering to the fields of science, technology, engineering, and math (STEM). While we promote STEM learning in and out of school for all kids, we are especially mindful of ensuring STEM learning opportunities for minorities, kids from low-income families, and girls—those who have traditionally been excluded from STEM learning opportunities, and thus eventually limited in terms of occupation.

The work we do is made possible by a team that is knowledgeable about both the content of educational policy issues and the communications specialties defined in our practice areas. While my team members can speak about education content at any given level, they also know how to communicate that knowledge simply and effectively—through a variety of vehicles to help the organizations we work with accelerate their own progress.

In creating this niche firm, Collaborative Communications, I have relied on the combination of my personal learning—in journalism, in nonprofit education, and in communications consulting. What I lacked at the point of the startup was formal business experience. What I learned on the business side of things, I learned by doing. And Collaborative is a successful mission-driven business that has been profitable every year since its inception.

We are the largest consulting firm in the country focused solely on education and learning. But, by design, we are not a huge company. We're a niche consulting firm, aimed at growing our revenue by roughly 10 percent each year. I did not create Collaborative to scale it. I created it to be high-touch. To build deep and lasting relationships with the people in our industry who value providing educational opportunity to minority children as a way of advancing our citizenry and democracy. Our values as an organization have truly become embedded in our business practices and in our business model, and I consider that key to our success.

It's been our goal to remain niche, and it has been our model to remain a boutique firm focused on the quality of the work we deliver—the development of beautiful products, websites, reports, and other digital tools.

We look to certain quality indicators to evaluate our work, and the most important of those centers on the importance of building relationships. Last year, for instance, 86 percent of our business came from repeat customers. So we know how important it is to deliver high-quality results each and every time. It's a lot easier to sustain and grow a current client than to go find a new one.

> *We know how important it is to deliver high-quality results each and every time. It's a lot easier to sustain and grow a current client than to go find a new one.*

Relationally, we have found that education in this country is a relatively insular business. Word of mouth is extremely important; what people say about their experience with us will lead either to the next business opportunity or to the next networking opportunity. If a project or engagement doesn't go well, we'll be looking at a series of stop signs.

We remain laser focused on customer service. Even in a relatively narrow field like education, we face a great deal of competition. It's easy for any client to find someone else who at least says they'll provide the same thing we do.

What's critical is that our team members demonstrate not only that they can develop creative deliverables but also that they care about the organizations we're working with—their people, their missions, their specific objectives.

Another key to our success has been our intentional focus on growing leadership capacity within our team. Moving up the ladder is not a matter of seat time. It's based on specific skills development, the consistent delivery of quality products, and the confidence of clients and other team members. That ladder leads all the way to the top. And we're deliberate and intentional about helping people move up—rather than out.

We have a core team of about twenty, and our business model allows us to expand it by using a deep network of freelancers and subcontractors we've developed relationships with over time. Many of our people have been with us for years and have served in many different roles and capacities. Multiple people on this team have held two, three, or even more positions, and have doubled their salaries—or more than doubled them—since they've started with us.

Our constant readiness as a team to conquer the next horizon—and then the next and the next—has helped us both to remain relevant over the years and to expand our reach. Originally our work was really focused on kindergarten through twelfth grade. We soon expanded into out-of-school learning and after school, then to early learning and what happens in pre-K. Over the past several years, we've expanded to focus beyond high school: We've developed a core business in college access and success and connections to the workforce. We now work directly with community colleges and post-secondary universities.

This follows the trends in the education space—to think about education as a significant pipeline from early learning all the way to college graduation and then into career. The language in the education space is to focus on preparing kids for college, career, and life.

In the early days at Collaborative, internet usage was really just starting to become pervasive. So during those initial years, we were strongly focused on the writing quality of our reports and other publications. My own history as a writer was at the core of this priority.

As technology has advanced, we haven't let go of that core focus on writing as a craft. We still produce significant publications, but quality writing and content development are now central to the digital practice we've created. This is an area of continual focus and growth for us: we often find we're ahead of educators in their use of technology.

While we continue to grow and evolve with our industry's changing needs, we've also found that we're cycling back to our main purpose in starting the organization: knowledge management. The volume of information in the world doubles yearly, and there is a pressing need to analyze that information, make sense of it, and get it into the hands of those who need it.

> **The volume of information in the world doubles yearly, and there is a pressing need to analyze that information, make sense of it, and get it into the hands of those who need it.**

The ability to help people make sense of the cacophony of data and information surrounding them is a thread that runs through everything we do. Even in the digital space, school districts and governments are continuously putting out a wealth of information, but very few people can understand and act on it.

Our work—fostering meetings in which people can learn from one another, positioning messages so they're more accessible to the public, data visualization, and so on—is really about creating a synthesis of information, making it compelling and meaningful, and most of all, making it actionable.

By running a for-profit with a mission, we have the opportunity to experience work that's doubly rewarding: It's needed and it's always focused on learning. We have been profitable financially. We've also had the opportunity to see our work actually help move the needle for people and organizations. We're doing well by doing good. Our founding mission—to take complex information and use it to move organizations to action—still guides everything we do. As we evolve, our values remain relevant.

CPSIA information can be obtained
at www.ICGtesting.com
Printed in the USA
FFHW010127260919
55214349-60941FF